North Wales Scrambles

North Wales Scrambles

Author Garry Smith

Design Garry Smith and Gav McGrath

Cover Gav McGrath

Photographs Garry Smith

Printed by Gomer Press... in Wales

Published by Northern Edge Books July 2014

Distribution Cordee www.cordee.co.uk

ISBN 978-0-9929692-0-2

reprinted June 2016

Any activity in the mountains carries with it a danger of personal injury or worse. Participants in these activities should be aware of and accept these risks and be responsible for their own actions. The information in this guide is given in good faith but cannot be taken as fact. It is essential that individuals make judgements for themselves. The author and publisher can accept no liability for damage to property nor for personal injury or death resulting from the use of this publication.

© Garry Smith 2014 All rights reserved. No Part of this publication may be reproduced, stored in or introduced into a retrieval system, or transmitted, in any form or by any means (electronic, mechanical, photocopying, recording or otherwise), without the prior written permission of the author.

Preface

Preface I am reluctant to define scrambling. It's something enjoyed in so many different ways, by so many different people. This book is my take on it.

Within the book you'll find descriptions of 50 of the best scrambling routes in North Wales. The choice of scrambles is purely personal. All the well-known classics have been included. The rest are simply the most enjoyable. They are ones that lead you to the other places - to the lonely cwms, the high neglected faces, and to obscure and funky little ridges. Places where you might otherwise never go.

Deciding on how much information to put in the descriptions wasn't easy. This guide had to be for everyone. As a friend advised, too much detail has the potential to 'overwhelm the inexperienced and to take away the voyage of discovery for the capable'. Hopefully I've struck a balance.

This book hasn't ended up as I thought it would. It's more personal than originally anticipated. Maybe that's down to all the good company I've had on the hill, the conversation, the chit chat, the out-there, the freedom, the fluidity, the exploring, being unencumbered... oh no, there I go starting to define scrambling, just when I said I wouldn't.

GS
July 2014

Acknowledgements

Acknowledgements During the hundreds of times ferreting around in the mountains, researching for this book, I've rarely been alone. I've had the company of some really ace people. They've shared their knowledge, given their perspective and ensured the book was fun and worthwhile. Thanks to -

Catrin Smith, Misha Lynden, George Smith, Mark Lynden, Rob Samuel, Miranda Grant, Dave Noddings, Gav McGrath, Eden Potter, Ric Potter, Emma Twyford, Tania Scotland, Steve Worth, Ben Lawes, Rob Collister, Tony Loxton, Dave Lees, Stevie Butterworth, Dominic Fawcett, John Redhead, Pimp Hey, Martyn Eade, Aaron Harris, Paul James, Matt Hawkins, Streaky Desroy, Kat Dunbar, Lou Lawrence, Paul Dickson, Libby Peter, Jason Wilkes, Ali Thomas, Nigel Shepherd, Zoe Wood, Konrad Doyle, Ryan Newman, James Whitmore, Ruth Bevan, Sheila van Lieshout, Sarah Ridgway, Robin Thomas, Ian Ridgway, Math Roberts, Sion Williams, Steph Evans, Calum Muskett, Derek Smith, Toby Keep, Mark 'Fluff' Taylor, Chris Wright, Anne Robertson, Tim Neill and Kath James.

For proof reading and scrutinising, there's additional thanks to Mark Lynden, Libby Peter, Anne Robertson, George Smith and James Whitmore.

For help in getting around the quirks of publishing software, there's yet more thanks to Mark Lynden. Also diolch to Emrys Roberts, Arfon Davis and Iestyn Lloyd for their frequent techy assistance. Simon Panton provided invaluable publishing and printing advice and Nigel Shepherd shared what he knew about photography stuff. Gav McGrath was thankfully always just an email away whenever help was needed with the design.

Ian Hey was the man of the maps and I'm massively appreciative of his attention to detail (now open for commissions as 'Hey Cartographics').

Thanks also to Brian, Sheila and Milo Cottam for providing the perfect writing environment during the winter months. And finally, and most importantly, thanks to Tan and Tomos for their continuous encouragement.

GS

Contents

Introduction

Area covered by the guide	09
Transport	09
Area map	10
Accommodation	12
Amenities	12
Using the route descriptions	13
Grading Scrambles	14
Maps	14
Weather and conditions	15
Equipment	15
Skills	18
What to do in an emergency	18
Access	19
The National Park	19

The Scrambles

Moel Siabod

01	Southeast Ridge - Daear Ddu	21

Carnedd Dafydd

02	Llech Ddu Spur (Crib Lem)	25

Tryfan Bach

03	Little Tryfan Arête	29

Tryfan

		33
04	South Rib Scramble	41
05	South Gully	43
06	Pinnacle Scramble	47
07	Little and North Gullies	51
08	North Buttress	53
09	Nor' Nor' Grooves	57

Contents

- **10** Nor' Nor' Buttress Scramble — 59
- **11** Bastow Buttress Scramble — 63
- *The Eastern Traverse Path* — 65
- **12** North Ridge — 67
- **13** Milestone Buttress Scramble — 71
- **14** Milestone Gully — 73
- **15** Wrinkled Tower — 75
- **16** West Face Direct — 79
- **17** South Ridge — 83

Glyder Fach Main Cliff — 87
- **18** Bristly Ridge — 93
- **19** Chasm Face Route — 97
- **20** Main Gully — 99
- **21** East Gully Ridge — 103
- **22** Hawks Nest Buttress Scramble — 105
- **23** Dolmen Ridge — 109

Glyders - Cwm Bochlwyd
- **24** Y Gribin — 113
- **25** Y Gribin True Start — 115

Cwm Idwal and Cwm Cneifion — 117
- **26** Cneifion Arête — 123
- **27** Tower Rib — 127
- **28** Seniors Gully — 129
- **29** Seniors Ridge Direct Approach — 133
- **30** Idwal Staircase — 135
- **31** Idwal Buttress & Continuation — 137
- **32** East Arête — 141
- **33** East Ridge of Y Garn — 145

Pen yr Ole Wen - Nant Ffrancon
- **34** Pinnacle Ridge — 149

Contents

Foel-goch - Nant Ffrancon
- **35** South Arête - Foel-goch ... 151
- **36** North Arête - Foel-goch ... 155

Carnedd y Filiast - Nant Ffrancon
- **37** Atlantic Ridge ... 159

Glyder Fawr - Llanberis Pass
- **38** Bryants Gully ... 163

Dinas Mot - Llanberis Pass
- **39** Jammed Boulder Gully ... 167

Crib Goch and Crib y Ddysgl ... 171
- **40** East Ridge of Crib Goch ... 175
- **41** North Ridge of Crib Goch ... 179
- **42** Main Ridge of Crib Goch ... 183
- *The Fox's Path* ... 186
- **43** Crib y Ddysgl ... 187
- **44** Clogwyn y Person Arête ... 191
- **45** Cwm Glas Spur ... 195
- **46** Llechog Buttress ... 199

Snowdon / Lliwedd
- **47** Y Gribin ... 203
- **48** Lliwedd Traverse ... 207
- **49** Bilberry Terrace Scramble ... 211

Mynydd Mawr
- **50** Sentries Ridge - Mynydd Mawr ... 215

Classic Link-ups ... 219
- Snowdon Horseshoe ... 219
- Cwm Bochlwyd Horseshoe ... 219
- Cwm Uchaf Circuit ... 219
- Northern Cwms of the Glyders ... 220

Llanberis High Street

Coffee in Brynrefail

Introduction

Area covered by the guide All the routes described in this guide are found within a small area in the north of the Snowdonia National Park. It is a landscape of rugged mountains connected by high ridges and dramatic hanging valleys. At its widest point, the area is little more than 20km across, and it is a mere 15km between its most northerly and southerly points. Both the north and west coastlines are only a short distance away, with the sea clearly visible from many of the area's summits.

The majority of the scrambles are concentrated in just two mountain ranges; the Glyders (Glyderau in Welsh) and the Snowdon (Yr Wyddfa) Group. Both ranges rise to over 1000m and are by far the most complex and impressive within the National Park. The handful of remaining routes are located close by; in the southwest quarter of the rolling Carneddau range and on the outlying peaks of Moel Siabod and Mynydd Mawr.

In previous centuries, slate quarrying and mining were major local industries. They have left a legacy of derelict quarries and ruined mine buildings scattered around the mountains. These are a crucial piece of the heritage of Snowdonia and now seem a part of the natural fabric of the landscape. Many have become a habitat to a wide diversity of wildlife.

Transport There is no shying away from the fact that the best way to get around is by car. Parking is rarely an issue. The exception being the Llanberis Pass during peak holiday periods, when an alternative park-and-ride service operates from the nearby village of Nant Peris. The most convenient parking location for each scramble is given in its approach description.

Using public transport is not easy or straightforward. The region is sparsely populated and the few bus services that exist are generally geared around local needs rather than those of the tourist. However, during the summer months a useful tourist bus service travels around the foot of the Snowdon range, linking to the Ogwen Valley and all the villages mentioned in this guide. Search for 'Snowdon Sherpa' to download a current timetable.

There is a good hitching culture around the region's mountain roads, with both locals and tourists happy to pick up people thumbing for a lift. It is surprisingly easy to catch rides along the Ogwen and Mymbyr Valleys, and up and down the Llanberis Pass. In effect, this links Llanberis to Bethesda in one large arc and makes it easy for those who don't have a vehicle to reach the roadside starting points of all but one of the scrambling venues.

Introduction

Accommodation If you'd like to stay in the local vicinity, Llanberis makes a good base. It has a range of accommodation and cafes catering specifically for outdoor tourism. Capel Curig has three long-established and popular hotels, along with a contemporary hostel and a few cafes. Slightly further afield and more twee, Betws-y-Coed and Beddgelert cater for the traditional tourist and have a large number of old-style hotels and guesthouses.

The area's campsites are basic but in great locations. Particularly good are those in the Ogwen Valley to the east of Tryfan, and in Nant Peris. There are more in Capel Curig, Nant Gwynant and on the outskirts of Llanberis. None of these sites require booking, just turn up and pitch. Wild camping is possible anywhere in the mountains so long as you stay on designated CROW land, are discreet and keep well away from residential properties.

Youth hostel (YHA) accommodation is well represented. The Idwal and Pen-y-pass hostels are stunningly located in the Ogwen Valley and Llanberis Pass. The Snowdon Ranger and Bryn Gwynant hostels are also in beautiful spots. Closer to amenities are the Llanberis and Betws-y-Coed hostels. If you prefer to stay in a foisty, old-school type bunkhouse, you're in luck, they still exist. Thankfully there's been a recent emergence of contemporary backpacker accommodation, and at a fine standard too. Good local examples are in Capel Curig, Llanberis and Dinorwig.

If you have your own vehicle it's feasible to stay anywhere in the northern half of the National Park and be within 45 minutes drive time to the scrambling venues. There are many good B&Bs, holiday cottages and quirky hotels tucked away in the valleys and along the coastline of North Wales. Finding these places is easy enough to do online.

Amenities There are convenience stores in every village with the exceptions of Rhyd Ddu and Waunfawr. Many of these shops open late. Bethesda has a small supermarket that is open from 6am to 11pm, seven days a week. The nearest major supermarkets are on the outskirts of Bangor and Caernarfon, or in Porthmadog if you are based more towards the centre of the National Park.

There are cafes in most villages but only in Llanberis and Capel Curig are you reliably able to score an early breakfast. Evening meals are available virtually everywhere in the summer months, less so during the winter. Most places will have stopped taking orders by 8.30pm. There are curry houses in Bethesda, Llanberis and on the A4086 towards Caernarfon, which continue serving

Introduction

much later. Great pubs are rare but not impossible to find. Online reviews will give the best indication of tourist-friendly establishments.

Well-stocked and helpful independent outdoor shops can be found in Llanberis and Capel Curig. The staff at these shops will freely give reliable advice on mountain conditions. The more familiar high street chains are all clustered in Betws-y-Coed.

Three local petrol stations are open 24 hours a day. These are located on the A5 approximately 4km northwest of Bethesda, on the A4244 approximately 2km northeast of Brynrefail and at the eastern end of Betws-y-Coed. Cashpoints (ATMs) can be found within most convenience stores, although 24-hour machines are only available in Llanberis, Bethesda and Betws-y-Coed.

Using the route descriptions The order in which the scrambles appear in the guide is purely down to their location. Routes that are geographically isolated, such as the Llech Ddu Spur (2), are described individually. Where there is a concentration of routes on one particular cliff or within a naturally defined area, such as Cwm Idwal and Cwm Cneifion, their descriptions have been grouped together into sections. These sections have a common introduction and where possible, try to avoid too much repetition of approach descriptions and descent options. Within each section, routes are listed following a convention of left to right when viewed from the valley floor.

The terms *left* and *right* refer to when you're facing a cliff. For other situations, the sensible Kiwi mountaineering terms of *true left* and *true right* have been used - the true right bank of a stream is the right bank when looking downstream. Mountain features are described using the most commonly used and widely understood terminology, regardless of language, such as cwm, saddle and couloir.

For each scramble, there is a brief description of a nearby or interesting descent route. There are also suggestions of where you can go next, such as an exceptional viewpoint, or the further scrambles that are possible for a longer mountain day.

This is a scrambling book and it doesn't have pretentions of being anything else. Rock type is described using useful and easy to understand adjectives, such as smooth or rough and quick-drying or greasy. On only a few occasions are accurate geological names used. For example, a boulder

Introduction

may be described as displaying a quartz streak, on the assumption that the distinctive white appearance of quartz is universally recognized. If you'd like to know how geology has shaped the landscape of North Wales, or whether the rock you're scrambling over is dolerite or rhyolite, get hold of Paul Gannon's informative book *Rock Trails Snowdonia*.

Mountain flora is also described in very simplistic terms. It is assumed that most people can visualise the difference between a grassy hillside and a heather-covered hillside. If a gully or ledge is overgrown with an abundance of different plant life it is simply described as being vegetated. The term boggy implies there's a likelihood of getting your feet wet. There are a number of good books available detailing the plant life of the British mountains, one specific to North Wales is Mike Raine's *Nature of Snowdonia*.

Grading scrambles The routes have been graded using a simple, progressive system with three levels of technical difficulty and seriousness.

Grade 1   Easy scrambles, within the capability of any adventurous mountain walker.

Grade 2   Interesting scrambles, where scrambling or mountaineering experience is essential.

Grade 3   Hard scrambles, which can be sustained and committing, and where it is not unusual to encounter sections of VDiff rock climbing.

These are further subdivided by the use of '+' to denote a particularly hard or serious scramble for the grade, and '-' to denote a relatively easy scramble for the grade or where any difficulties are short-lived.

All scrambles can be exposed and are possible to fall off regardless of their grade. If you are unsure of your ability or new to the game, start with the easier and more popular routes.

Maps The guide is designed to be used in conjunction with an OS 1:25000 Explorer Series map. The route descriptions are written on the basis that you'll be carrying this type of map. If you're more comfortable using a GPS, grid references are given for the starting points of routes. No matter how slick a GPS is to use, keep with the habit of also carrying a map and compass.

Introduction

The off-the-shelf Ordnance Survey *OL 17 Snowdon Explorer Map* covers the vast majority of the area and 49 of the scrambles. The *OL 18 Harlech Explorer Map* covers the remaining scramble on the outlying peak of Moel Siabod. Bespoke 1:25000 maps of exactly the area covered in this guide can be purchased online at www.ordnancesurvey.co.uk

The maps in this book are to scale and very accurate, but are only intended to help planning and for armchair use. A red dashed line corresponds to an approach route outlined in the description but it may not necessarily translate to a tangible footpath or visible track on the ground. A darker dashed line represents an established path or track that will be visible on the ground.

Weather and conditions Scrambling can be done all year round and in most weathers. Undoubtedly it is most enjoyable during those magic periods of high pressure when the rock is dry and there is little wind (which occurs more often than you might think). With a bit of caution low-grade scrambles are fine to tackle in wet weather, especially the popular classics, which tend to be worn free of lichen and less slippy. If a route is sheltered or quick-drying after wet weather, this is often indicated in its introduction.

Any scramble would be a totally different proposition when the mountains are covered in snow and ice. This scenario is a complete game-changer, requiring winter climbing equipment and a whole new set of skills. Strong winds can also make it too dangerous to go scrambling. Good, informative mountain weather forecasts are freely available with the touch of a screen. Making a decision based on these forecasts is the tricky part that only gets easier with experience. Each scramble's aspect and elevation are given at the beginning of its description and can be used to figure out whether the route is a suitable choice in the prevailing weather. If in doubt, play to caution and stick with something easy.

Equipment A sure way to scupper a good scramble is to carry a heavy pack. It goes against the grain of moving freely in the mountains. Dress according to the forecasted weather and for the style in which you're scrambling. When running a scramble on a nice summer's day there may be little need to carry anything other than a wind-proof. For a high-level scramble on an iffy autumnal day, it would be unwise to set off without a waterproof shell and a few additional warm layers.

Yee-haa... Konrad Doyle on **East Arête**

Streaky Desroy trailing a rope for the team on a difficult section of **Hawks Nest Buttress Scramble**

Introduction

The choice of footwear is down to personal preference. Nothing beats the freedom and responsiveness of wearing lightweight approach shoes. Fell shoes are also liberating but can be a bit dicey on harder scrambles, where a flat-edged sole comes in handy. Traditional stiff-soled boots certainly help keep your feet dry and provide essential warmth during the colder months, but often feel over-the-top on warm summer days. The claimed benefit of ankle support is questionable and they can feel clumsy on rocky terrain, especially if you're not accustomed to wearing them. If boots are your thing, very lightweight alpine boots are regarded as the best choice for year-round scrambling.

What technical gear, if any, to take on a scramble is an endless debate. There is no correct answer. The route you intend to do, your level of experience and the mountain conditions forecast for the day will all influence your decision. On easy scrambles, a 15m 'skinny' rope is sometimes carried within a team for emergency use. Although harder scrambles are frequently done without the use of a rope, a short length is often carried along with a small amount of rock climbing gear. This is particularly so with less experienced teams and is almost universal on the more serious routes, such as Jammed Boulder Gully (39) and Bilberry Terrace (49), or when weather conditions are hard going.

If carrying rock climbing gear, it would be excessive to take a rope any longer than 30m. Likewise, anything bigger than an 'alpine rack' is superfluous - a set of nuts, a few cams, two or three extenders and some slings should be all that is needed to protect the stiffer sections of virtually every scramble within this guide. If none of this makes sense, see the following skills section.

It is not common practice to wear helmets on grade 1 scrambles. However, if you fall off any scramble, no matter how easy, a helmet would undoubtedly reduce the risk of a serious head injury. A lot of scrambling terrain is loose and gnarly, and wearing a helmet is always a sensible precaution. Make your own judgement.

The most important stuff to pack for any scramble should include a windproof or waterproof, a map and compass, a mobile phone, a basic first aid kit and a headtorch. Have good justification before leaving any of these behind. Go light but be well prepared.

Introduction

Skills Any reasonably fit person can enjoy the easier scrambles of North Wales. The ability to scramble is natural and intuitive. It rarely requires any formal training. So long as you, or somebody with you, has some general mountain-walking nous and can navigate using a map and compass, there is every reason to just go for it. If you lack confidence in your route finding ability, start by picking scrambles that follow a strong natural line, like a ridge.

Stepping up from the easier scrambles is a different ball game, especially if you lack a mountaineering or rock climbing background. Terrain can often be steep, insecure and loose, requiring all sorts of tricky judgements. Without experience or the knowledge of rock climbing techniques, this can be well scary. There are a number of locally based instructors who can equip you with the skills for tackling harder scrambles. Many also offer guided scrambling days. Look at www.themic.org.uk for their contact details.

What to do in an Emergency Amongst hill-goers in the UK there is a strong tradition of self-reliance. If there has been an accident and there is any possibility of limping safely back to the valley under your own steam, you should choose this option. This is preferable, as the people who will most likely come to your rescue will be volunteers. The mountain rescue teams in North Wales comprise un-paid locals who give up their free time to provide a highly trained and always on-call rescue service. It would be irresponsible and perhaps immoral to unnecessarily request their assistance. If you would like to support this service, consider making the occasional donation.

In the event of an accident on the hill, the first thing to do is pause and take time to rationally evaluate the situation. If there is no sensible option other than to get help, call 999 (or 112) and ask for the police. When connected to the local police, then ask for mountain rescue. Have ready the details of your location (preferably a grid reference) and be prepared to calmly explain what has happened.

The above only touches upon what to do if there is an accident. Being familiar with emergency procedures in the mountains could save a life or help a rescue run smoothly. Good practical advice is available in Kath Wills' comprehensive book *Outdoor First Aid*. Better still; go on one of her courses.

The nearest hospital emergency department is at Ysbyty Gwynedd Hospital on the outskirts of Bangor, LL57 2PW (558 703), 01248 384 384.

Introduction

Access All the routes in this guide are on land designated as 'open access' under the Countryside and Rights of Way Act (CROW). This assures the right to walk anywhere without having to stick to footpaths. Open access land, or CROW land as it is sometimes called, is clearly indicated on the 1:25000 OS Explorer map using a beige tint and an opaque orange border. Approaches to three scrambling routes briefly travel across land that is not 'open access'. However, the land is crossed using footpaths with a public right of way. The approaches are to the Southeast Ridge of Moel Siabod (1), the Llech Ddu Spur (2) and Sentries Ridge (50) on Mynydd Mawr.

With rights come responsibilities - Aim to leave the mountain environment as you find it by keeping your impact to a minimum. Respect the fact that others work and farm on the land, and be careful not to damage walls or fences. Be particularly sensitive around lambing time and always keep dogs under control. Have some consideration when you're near residential properties. In a nutshell, just don't do the sort of stuff that would nark anyone.

The people in Wales do not have the same freedom of movement as that enjoyed in Scotland. At the time of writing, the prospect of legislation to grant better access to the Welsh mountains and waterways has all but evaporated. Intense and orchestrated lobbying from landowners, farming organisations and conservative groups has pressurised the Welsh Government into retracting their promise of improving access to the outdoors.

The National Park Snowdonia was designated a National Park in 1951, and as such became 'one of Britain's breathing places'. However, don't take your enjoyment of these mountains for granted. The conservation of the park's natural beauty and the protection of its landscape for future generations seem to be threatened by the very people who have been entrusted to run it.

The current Park Authority appears to hold agricultural land use in higher regard than everything else. This may seem an odd place to air these views but I feel it's important. The Park Authority needs to be reminded of its founding principles, particularly the high value to be placed on open-air recreation. Visitors to Snowdonia shouldn't be seen as a problem to be managed; they are one of the primary reasons for the park's existence. Enjoy your time in North Wales, but be aware, it would be tragic if we all stood by and let Snowdonia become a National Park in name only.

Catrin Smith, Misha Lynden and Chita taking it easy on Moel Siabod's **South East Ridge**

01

Moel Siabod's **South East Ridge**

South East Ridge - Daear Ddu

Moel Siabod

01

Grade	1-
Area	Mymbyr Valley
Aspect	Southeast (600m)
Approach	60 mins (713 546)

Simple scrambling with a wide-open feel. Moel Siabod (872m) sits on its own, separated from the other mountains by the wide Mymbyr Valley. It is high enough, and sufficiently far away, to offer views spanning all the mountain ranges of North Wales. The route ascends a shapely but very easy ridge on the south side of the mountain. Every small rocky step can be taken on or bypassed at will. There is no exposure, just an immense feeling of space normally attributable to bigger hills. Although not a short outing, it is a good choice for adventurous nippers and a very good scramble to run.

Approach Head south from Capel Curig along the A5, towards Betws-y-Coed. Continue for two kilometres until the Bryn Glo carpark (736 571), just beyond Pont Cyfyng. Park here or in the small lay-by 100m back along the A5.

Walk 200m northwest along the A5 until the junction with a minor road on the left. Head south along the minor road for 120m, crossing the Afon Llugwy river, to reach the start of a steep, tarmacked vehicle track on the right. Head up the track for approximately 225m, as far as a sharp right turn. Ignore the turn and continue straight ahead on a footpath diversion.

The footpath rejoins the track further up the hill, close to the highest dwelling. Cross a stile and head southwest up a grassy cart track. Moel Siabod is directly ahead, with the southeast ridge forming the left-hand skyline. At the end of the cart track a footpath veers to the left, passing a small lake, before rising gently to an abandoned quarry.

Pass the quarry hole on the left (south) then veer back right, to pick up an eroded path. The path climbs southwest, over peaty ground, to a wide shoulder overlooking Cwm y Foel. The base of the southeast ridge is at the far side of the cwm.

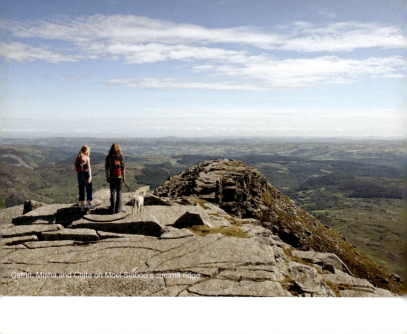
Catrin, Misha and Chita on Moel Siabod's summit ridge

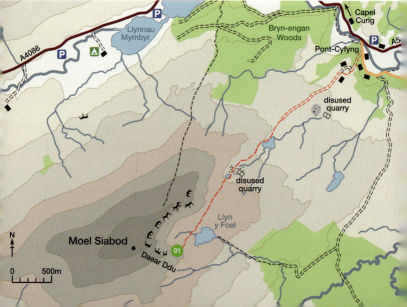

Moel Siabod — South East Ridge - Daear Ddu

More often than not, the floor of Cwm y Foel is boggy. Passing Llyn y Foel on its south side will keep your feet dry. Passing the lake on its north side, the more tempting direct way, is sometimes a risk. On reaching the southwest corner of the cwm, the crest of the ridge can be gained at a number of places along its broad base.

Description Pick a way up the ridge. It is always easier on the left and more entertaining on the right. At two-thirds height, the route changes its character, with Moel Siabod feeling more like a mountain than a hill. The summit trig point only comes into view when nearing the very top of the ridge. There is a well-constructed, circular stone shelter a few metres from the summit.

Descents or where next The best and most direct descent is to head northeast, along the more or less level summit ridge. At the end of the level rocky section, continue in the same direction, down a broad ridge; rocky at first, then grassy. At the base of the grassy ridge, veer slightly to the true right, allowing yourself to be funnelled steeply downhill through a series of wide runnels.

As the runnels peter out, veer right again, across open ground, to meet with the cart track used on the approach. Follow the track back to Pont Cyfyng.

There is a more established and straightforward descent route if required. A path drops obliquely down the hillside in a north-northeasterly direction from the summit. At the bottom of the path, at the river, turn right and follow a forestry track east through Bryn-engan woods, back to the start point at Pont Cyfyng. This is an easy and fast descent route to run.

Rob Samuel and Miranda Grant tip toe along a narrowing on the **Llech Ddu Spur**

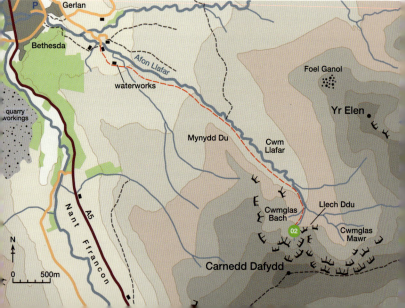

Llech Ddu Spur (Crib Lem)

Carnedd Dafydd

02

Grade	1
Area	Carneddau
Aspect	North (715m)
Approach	80 mins (665 635)

A top-drawer scramble in a dramatic mountain setting. The route follows a devious path to gain the crest of a striking ridge, which is perched above Cwm Llafar; a long, secluded valley with a feeling of wildness that is unsurpassed anywhere in Wales. The scrambling is exposed but always easy, and always on reliable rock. Good approach tracks and access onto the high, rolling ground of the Carneddau peaks, also make this an attractive scramble to run.

Approach The Carneddau, an area covering nearly 200 square kilometres, is the biggest of the mountain ranges in North Wales. They extend north from the Ogwen Valley and east from the Nant Ffrancon. Carnedd Dafydd is located in the southwest corner of the range, with the Llech Ddu Spur sitting high on its north face, hidden from both major valleys. It is logistically sensible, and an integral part of the experience, to approach the scramble from the northwest, along the secluded Cwm Llafar.

Start from Gerlan, an area that was once a separate village on the eastern edge of Bethesda. Gerlan is best reached from a crossroads on the A5, just south of Bethesda. At the kinked crossroads, turn east and head up the Braichmelyn Road. Continue over a river and up a steep hill until a further crossroads. Turn sharply right and continue into Gerlan. Parking spaces are limited so please park sensibly with consideration for residents.

It is also possible to park in Bethesda. Turn left immediately after crossing the river on the Braichmelyn Road. Park here, on this non-residential stretch of road (630 663). A footpath, starting on the opposite side of the Braichmelyn Road, adjacent to the bridge and marked on a map, heads east up to Gerlan. There is very little extra walking involved by parking here.

The striking line of the **Llech Ddu Spur** seen from Mynydd Du

A scoot across to Pen yr Ole Wen from the top of the **Llech Ddu Spur**

Carnedd Dafydd **Llech Ddu Spur (Crib Lem)**

Walk up the narrow lane, Gerlan Road, that heads southeast out of the village. At the end of the lane, turn right and cross a road bridge over the Afon Llafar. Continue past the waterworks sign, then cross a stile to the right of the gate marked 'private'. Head up the left side of the field, skirting around the waterworks.

Cross another stile at the top left corner of the field. Turn right and follow a well-trodden route through old enclosures towards more open ground. Occasional marker posts help confirm direction, as does the Afon Llafar, which soon flows parallel to the path (100m to the left).

Less than a kilometre after passing the waterworks, the path becomes a narrow, well-constructed track. This runs straight up the right-hand side of Cwm Llafar. After 3km the track arrives at a collection of large boulders beneath Llech Ddu; a 100m high, steep pyramidal crag that looms over the valley floor. The white quartz bands, on the shoulder above the crag, mark the start of the Llech Ddu Spur.

Skirt the edge of the boulder field to a path that zig-zags up the scree slope to the right of Llech Ddu. The path leads to a small hanging cwm, Cwmglas Bach, which nestles beneath the ragged northeast cliffs of Carnedd Dafydd.

Approximately 30m before reaching the steep headwall of the cwm (and when almost level with the base of the crag to your right), the path cuts back and left, up a gently rising, grassy ramp line. This distinctive ramp line leads to the shoulder above Llech Ddu and the quartz bands that mark the start of the scramble.

Description Scramble straight up from the shoulder, picking a way through short rock steps and runnels. The ridge soon narrows, with extremely steep grassy slopes on either side. Sticking to the rocky crest is the most fun. Otherwise, sidestep any obstacles using sneaky little detours on both the left and right flanks.

The ridge eventually merges into the summit dome. At this point it's worth turning around and appreciating what a magnificent line the route has taken. Continue easily to the summit.

The clean west facing slab of Tryfan Bach 03

Descent or where next The quickest descent from the summit of Carnedd Dafydd is to head northwest. An easy-to-follow track skirts around the top of Cwmglas Bach before descending the gently-angled ridge of Mynydd Du. The Cwm Llafar path is then followed back to Gerlan.

Before descending, a worthwhile side trip is to scoot across to Pen yr Ole Wen, for a panorama and a half. Head southwest over a long rocky saddle before swinging southeast to the summit cairn of Pen yr Ole Wen. It is easier to return Carnedd Dafydd by the same route before dropping to Gerlan.

Alternatively, for an excellent high-level ridge walk (or run), head east from Carnedd Dafydd's summit. This picks up the path that skirts around the head of Cwm Llafar before it swings north to the summit of Carnedd Llewelyn. From Carnedd Llewelyn, head northwest, across a broad saddle, to the outlying peak of Yr Elen. An easy descent of the rocky northwest flank leads to the rocky outcrop of Foel Ganol. From here, drop to the true left, over open ground, towards the Cwm Llafar path. There is a ford across the Afon Llafar (655 650), if you like dry feet.

Little Tryfan Arête

Tryfan Bach

03

Grade	3
Area	Ogwen Valley
Aspect	West (360m)
Approach	10 mins (671 601)

A quick scrambling hit or an exciting prelude to a bigger outing on Tryfan's East Face. The slab of Tryfan Bach is a huge expanse of gently-angled rock. Its surface is covered with friendly incut holds. It is also incredibly clean, with no loose rock and in a relatively sheltered location. As a consequence, Tryfan Bach is a very sociable and relaxed crag. An ascent of the left edge of the slab gives a short but excellent technical scramble... and with a bit of imagination, there's even a little summit. If you're passing through the Ogwen Valley, don't poo-poo the idea of a half-hour scramble stop. The route is remarkably quick to dry after any rain.

Approach Park at the roadside (674 604) just west of Gwern Gof Uchaf Campsite on the A5 Ogwen Valley road. Walk through the campsite and take the path on the left of the farmhouse. Cross the stile, turn right and walk west along the old Ogwen Road. After 50m, turn left up a footpath. Cross a stile and continue obliquely right, across the hillside, to the toe of the crag.

Description Start at the bottom left of the slab. Scramble up and left, across the top of the steep truncation, aiming for the left edge of the slab. Continue delicately up the edge for 25m to reach a ledge. A polished crack line, a few metres from the edge, provides an easier alternative.

Continue up the left edge, which is now more of an arête, to reach the top of the slab. Again, a polished crack, a few metres from the edge, provides an easier, protectable alternative line.

Follow a system of grooves rightwards, across the top of the crag, to a large grassy shoulder. Scramble up to the final steepening and enter a steep groove. Exit the groove via its right wall to reach the top of Tryfan Bach.

Dave Noddings starting up **Little Tryfan Arête**

Tryfan Bach **Little Tryfan Arête**

Descent or where next To return to the road, continue south along the broad heather-covered crest of Tryfan Bach. At the first practical opportunity, drop left (east) to meet the flagstone path coming out of Cwm Tryfan. Follow the path directly down to the campsite.

To return to the start of the scramble, continue along the crest of Tryfan Bach until it peters into the hillside, a short way before the fence. Drop right (west) into a runnel and follow a rough path, which leads back under the slab.

To reach any of the scrambles on Tryfan's East Face, continue along the crest of Tryfan Bach until just before the fence. Turn right (west) and follow the path on the right (north) side of the fence line. After 200m, the path enters a steep gully and climbs a paved staircase to reach the beginnings of the Heather Terrace; the prominent wide ramp that runs obliquely across the East Face. At the top of the gully, turn left (south) and follow any of a number of rough tracks, which all eventually converge to form the main Heather Terrace path. Individual approach descriptions for any of the East Face scrambles can be followed from this point.

The East Face of Tryfan seen from the A5 Ogwen Valley Road

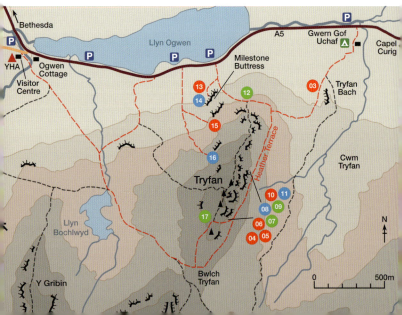

Tryfan

Ogwen Valley

04	South Rib Scramble	3
05	South Gully	3-
06	Pinnacle Scramble	3+
07	Little and North Gullies	1
08	North Buttress	2-
09	Nor' Nor' Grooves	1+
10	Nor' Nor' Buttress Scramble	3+
11	Bastow Buttress Scramble	2
12	North Ridge	1
13	Milestone Buttress Scramble	3
14	Milestone Gully	2-
15	Wrinkled Tower	3
16	West Face Direct	2+
17	South Ridge	1-

Tryfan (915m) is a beautiful mountain; from whichever direction it is viewed. Iconic even. It is shaped like a huge fin, with its crest running from north to south. The simple, almost classical silhouette hides a complex topography. Huge buttresses, deep gullies, hidden amphitheatres, endless rocky ribs and runnels, combine to produce a fascinating mountain playground. Fourteen scrambles are described but many more are possible among the nooks and crannies of this great looking peak.

Tryfan stands on its own, on the south side of the Ogwen Valley, projecting out from the main Glyders chain. It is separated from Glyder Fach (994m) by a col that dips by 200m. The central summit stands at over 600m above the valley floor but is only 1km from the road. This geographical isolation and marked steepness gives scrambling over Tryfan's tops a unique feeling of loftiness, of the kind not normally experienced in the more rounded surrounding hills.

The mountain's North Ridge is a true scrambling classic and should be on everybody's tick list. Rising straight from the road, it is so entertaining and absorbing that it can be done again and again. So many route variations exist on the broad lower half of the ridge that no two ascents ever feel the same.

Tryfan   Ogwen Valley

The South Ridge (17) is on the far side of the mountain, away from the road, and drops into Bwlch Tryfan; the col before Glyder Fach. It is only a third of the height of the North Ridge and much more benign. It is almost a 'baby scramble', providing a scenic, hands-on route to the summit, which is only a step up from a steep walk.

Three massive buttresses dominate the East Face. They are over 200m high and their tops denote the three summits of Tryfan. All the described East Face scrambles start from the **Heather Terrace**; the prominent wide ramp that runs obliquely across the face, rising from north to south. Each scramble is a proper mountaineering route. They are either natural or logical lines and all finish on a summit. The scale and complexities of the face can best be appreciated from the floor of Cwm Tryfan. It is worth the extra distance to descend via this cwm, particularly if there's good visibility.

The East Face receives sun throughout the morning and can be a warm suntrap even on mid-winter days. It provides shelter from all westerly air streams and can be spookily calm during the strongest of winds. The three described scrambles based around gully lines also provide shelter from southerly and northerly winds. The rock is generally clean, solid and with the exception of the narrower parts of gullies, dries quickly after wet weather.

The easier-angled West Face has a sense of vastness that is disproportionate to its true size. Its sprawling and broken nature undeservedly attracts few visitors. The face is covered in rambling rocky ribs and small outcrops, interspersed by acres of steep heather and the occasional impressive gully. Despite this discontinuity of rock, the scrambling is good, having an adventurous and 'away from it all' ambience. The rock quality on the ribs and outcrops is exceptional but needs care if you are exploring elsewhere. The face receives the sun from early afternoon onwards and is a lovely place to be on a summer's evening.

The Milestone Buttress is a notable Tryfan feature and could almost be classed as a roadside crag. It is an intricate little buttress located at the bottom left of the West Face, virtually at the foot of the North Ridge. Running away from the buttress on its eastern (left) side is a line of small, impenetrable cliffs. Its western side looks more inviting and consists of gently-angled slabs and sloping corners. Despite its friendly appearance, the buttress is mostly too hard a proposition for scrambling. The described Milestone Buttress Scramble (13) is one of only a few scrambles that manage to sneak across the crag without embracing too much difficulty.

Standing upright on Tryfan's summit are two large, angular monoliths known as **Adam and Eve**. They are 3m high, just over a metre apart and are clearly visible from the valley floor. There is an old tradition of first-time visitors jumping from one to the other. Easier said than done, as the presence of the East Face may be too intimidating.

Heather Terrace approach At its beginnings, on the right (north) side of the face, the terrace is little more than a poorly-defined sloping shelf. As it rises gently across the face, beneath the buttresses, it quickly develops into a wide, heather and rock covered gangway. There is a rough but easy to follow path along its entire length.

Towards its left end, the terrace slowly loses identity and merges into the mountainside. The terrace's rough path however, continues in the same direction before climbing up to Bwlch Tryfan. A short distance after passing beneath the South Buttress, a subsidiary track breaks off from the main terrace path and climbs to the col separating the South buttress and the Far South Peak.

For an easy approach to the terrace, park at the roadside (674 604) just west of Gwern Gof Uchaf Campsite on the A5 Ogwen Valley road. Walk through the campsite and take the path on the left of the farmhouse. Cross the stile, turn right and walk west along the old Ogwen Road. After 50m, turn left up a way-marked footpath. Cross a stile and continue obliquely right, across the hillside, to the slab of Tryfan Bach.

Continue past the slab and follow a rough path uphill, until just before a fence. Turn right (west) and follow the path on the right (north) side of the fence line. After 200m, the path enters a steep gully and climbs a paved staircase to reach the beginnings of the terrace. At the top of the gully, turn left (south) and follow any of a number of rough tracks, which all eventually converge to form the main Heather Terrace path.

A quicker but rougher approach to the terrace starts by leaving the road from the kissing gate (663 603) at the layby beneath the Milestone Buttress. Follow the path uphill, staying on the left of the wall, up to the highest stile. The stile is directly beneath the steep cliffs that run up and left from the Milestone Buttress.

The view to the east from Tryfan's South Summit

Sarah Leeds' variation on the traditional jump from Adam to Eve

Ogwen Valley Tryfan

From the stile the path heads left (east), picking its way up to a heather and boulder covered shoulder on the North Ridge. This is the lowest shoulder on the ridge and easily identifiable from the road. Contour round to the East Face, over uneven bouldery terrain, to meet with the beginnings of the terrace.

Tryfan descent options The quickest descent from Tryfan's summit (915m) is via the west flank route. Head northwest from Adam and Eve and drop into the bay just below the summit rise. From here, go straight down the well-used, rubble-filled depression running the length of the west face. At the bottom of the depression (750m contour), a paved path curves northwest down the steep grassy slopes.

For a more gentle descent, head down the South Ridge (17), passing the South Summit on its right (west), to reach a flattening before the rocky protrusion of the far south peak. This flattening, or col, is spanned by a stone wall with two stiles (strangely the wall is not shown on any map). From the flattening, head southwest to join the main Cwm Bochlwyd path,

Alternatively, from the flattening, drop down a scree slope on the east, veering slightly to the true left, to meet with the northern end of the Heather Terrace. If time allows, and visibility is good, continue down the scree slope to meet with the Cwm Tryfan path. The path leads back to the Ogwen Valley road, arriving at the Gwern Gof Uchaf campsite. This descent route offers excellent views of Tryfan's east face, from where the size and complexity of the buttresses can really be appreciated. It is highly recommended if you've just done a scramble on the face.

An atmospheric descent, and the quickest way of reaching the Heather Terrace for another east face scramble, starts from behind Adam and Eve, on their steep east side. From here, scramble down to the true right (southeast), towards South Gully to reach a well-worn terrace - the Eastern Traverse Path. Cut back to the true left and follow the scrambly path into the upper amphitheatre of North Gully (07). From the back of the amphitheatre, descend the easy scree path that zig-zags down the wide gully bed. At half height, directly above an appreciable steepening, branch off to the true right, into the much narrower Little Gully. A short but straightforward scramble, down the confined lower section of the gully, brings you out mid-way along the Heather Terrace.

Gav McGrath starting the exposed second rib on **South Rib Scramble**

South Rib Scramble

Tryfan East Face

04

Grade	3
Area	Ogwen Valley
Aspect	East (780m)
Approach	60 mins (664 592)

An entertaining scramble along an exposed but intermittent ridge line at the far end of the Heather Terrace. Although this is a very discontinuous scramble (it can be walked away from at just about any point), the difficulties are fun and don't feel too contrived. It's a good choice as a quick second route on the east face, being only a short distance from the col between the South Summit and the Far South Peak.

Approach Follow either of the approaches described on page 35 to gain the beginnings of the Heather Terrace, the prominent, wide ramp that runs obliquely across the East Face, rising from north to south.

Head up the terrace path. At first the actual terrace can be difficult to make out, but after a short rise, when the buttresses come into view, the terrace becomes an unmistakable feature; a wide heather and rock covered gangway running up the mountainside.

Cross the first gully, which is little more than a watercourse containing grass and stones, and continue underneath the first proper crags to a better-defined second gully. This is Bastow Gully, which has steep retaining walls and a uniform grassy bed littered with small blocks.

Continue up the terrace for a further 75m to Nor' Nor' Gully. Apart from curving to the left at mid-height, it is identifiable by a huge coffin shaped boulder lying 40m up the bed of the gully.

Approximately 75m further on is Green Gully, easily identified by 'GA' (Grooved Arête) scratched onto the rock 6m to the left of its entrance. It is less pronounced than the previous gullies and has no continuation beneath the Heather Terrace.

South Rib Scramble   Tryfan East Face

Continue up the terrace to reach the 4th significant gully, North Gully. It is narrower and steeper than the previous gullies, with a jammed block forming a cave at 40m up the bed of the gully.

Just beyond the entrance to North Gully, a long, flat-topped boulder sits in the middle of the Heather Terrace, splitting the terrace path. A further 120m along the terrace is the final significant gully, South Gully, which separates South and Central Buttresses. It is identifiable by its broad entrance with a pinnacle standing on the left-hand side. Jammed blocks choke a constriction 30m up the bed of the gully.

A short distance beyond South Gully the terrace path divides. Follow the higher path for 35m to where it crosses a patch of cracked slabs. Directly above is a grassy bay with a steep rocky rib on either side. At half height, there are a couple of small plinths of rock spanning the vegetated gap between the two ribs. This bay is the start to South Rib Scramble.

Description Start by scrambling up into the central bay, or step into the upper part of the bay from high up on either bounding rib. From the top of the bay, continue energetically along a rib, over flakes and pinnacles, for approximately 40m until it merges into a platform consisting of jumbled boulders.

Head right, up a sloping gangway towards a second rib, but after 3m stop in a small bay directly beneath a block-filled chimney. Climb the chimney and exit through a slot, then turn right and follow a second sloping gangway to the base of the rib. Ascend the rib's exposed crest to a notch.

The direct continuation of the rib above the notch is too difficult. Instead, walk 15m left across a grassy bay and enter a chimney formed under huge perched blocks. Thrutch up the chimney and exit rightwards (if you've managed to stay facing uphill!) to emerge on a platform, back on the crest of the second rib.

Continue upwards across the intermittent large blocks that constitute the now vague rib. At the end of the line of blocks is a third rib, lying in the same line as the previous rib and having a clean nose of rock at its base. Gain the rib on its right and then continue up its crest, with a short detour into a chimney at half height, to arrive below a steep wall. Climb the wall by a hard groove slightly to the left, or bypass the wall altogether by traversing left. Either way leads easily to the South Summit. Descent options are described on page 37.

South Gully

Tryfan East Face

05

Grade	3-
Area	Ogwen Valley
Aspect	East (780m)
Approach	55 mins (665 593)

An atmospheric journey through two large amphitheatres that nestle between the towering walls of South Buttress and the steep terraces of Central Buttress. The route's main attraction is undoubtedly the impressive mountain architecture under which it passes. The floors of both amphitheatres are littered with loose rock and scree but the intervening rock steps provide some reasonable scrambling interest. Once the initial slabby barrier has been overcome, even though there are no easy escape routes, the overall difficulty drops to grade 2.

Approach Follow either of the approaches described on page 35 to gain the beginnings of the Heather Terrace, the prominent, wide ramp that runs obliquely across the east face, rising from north to south.

Head up the terrace path. At first the actual terrace can be difficult to make out, but after a short rise, when the buttresses come into view, the terrace becomes an unmistakable feature; a wide heather and rock covered gangway running up the mountainside.

Cross the first gully, which is little more than a watercourse containing grass and stones, and continue underneath the first proper crags to a better-defined second gully. This is Bastow Gully, which has steep retaining walls and a uniform grassy bed littered with small blocks.

Continue up the terrace for a further 75m to Nor' Nor' Gully. Apart from curving to the left at mid-height, it is identifiable by a huge coffin shaped boulder lying 40m up the bed of the gully.

Eden and Ric Potter safeguarding the initial slabby barrier to **South Gully**

Tryfan East Face — **South Gully**

Approximately 75m further on is Green Gully, easily identified by 'GA' (Grooved Arête) scratched onto the rock 6m to the left of its entrance. It is less pronounced than the previous gullies and has no continuation beneath the Heather Terrace.

Continue up the terrace to reach the 4th significant gully, North Gully. It is narrower and steeper than the previous gullies, with a jammed block forming a cave at 40m up the bed of the gully.

Just beyond the entrance to North Gully, a long, flat-topped boulder sits in the middle of the Heather Terrace, splitting the terrace path. A further 120m along the terrace is the final significant gully, South Gully, which separates South and Central Buttresses. It is identifiable by its broad entrance with a pinnacle standing on the left-hand side. Jammed blocks choke a constriction 30m up the bed of the gully.

Description Enter the gully and ascend smooth slabs on the right; the very smooth lower slab is desperate when wet, the upper slab is much easier and best climbed by its right-hand corner. Alternatively, scramble up the bed of the gully until underneath the chockstone. Then, with the aid of a jutting block, reach behind for a rightward leaning crack line and make some quick but secure moves to reach a ledge above the very smooth lower slab.

Above the slabs is a grassy area followed by a 4m high rock band extending across the gully and guarding the entrance to the main amphitheatre. Ascend this on its left-hand side by a series of natural rock steps.

Splitting the impressive main amphitheatre is a rib of rock, South Gully Rib. Scramble into the narrow gully on the left of the rib, continue to the end of the gully and exit steeply left into a grassy bay.

Follow a short scree path until confronted by a huge boulder, undercut on its front face. Go to the right of the boulder and escape from the resulting confines by some delightful stepped slabs on the right.

Continue up the gully to meet the final obstacle, a 10m high rib barring the entrance to the upper amphitheatre. Scramble up a steep groove on the right and break into the contrasting expanse of the amphitheatre. Gain the south ridge via a niche in the back wall of the amphitheatre or trend up and right to emerge near Adam and Eve. Descent options are described on page 37.

Gav McGrath bridging up the superb initial groove of **Pinnacle Scramble**

Pinnacle Scramble

Tryfan East Face

06

Grade	3+
Area	Ogwen Valley
Aspect	East (780m)
Approach	55 mins (665 593)

A very good scramble, probably the best on Tryfan's east face. It takes a weaving line up Central Buttress, sneaking through terrain historically claimed by rock climbers. There is nothing artificial about this route; it always seeks out the easiest passage rather than looking for difficulty. The scrambling is continually interesting with good, solid rock for its entire length. There are plenty of belays if required.

Approach Follow either of the approaches described on page 35 to gain the beginnings of the Heather Terrace, the prominent, wide ramp that runs obliquely across the East Face, rising from north to south.

Head up the terrace path. At first the actual terrace can be difficult to make out, but after a short rise, when the buttresses come into view, the terrace becomes an unmistakable feature; a wide heather and rock covered gangway running up the mountainside.

Cross the first gully, which is little more than a watercourse containing grass and stones, and continue underneath the first proper crags to a better-defined second gully. This is Bastow Gully, which has steep retaining walls and a uniform grassy bed littered with small blocks.

Continue up the terrace for a further 75m to Nor' Nor' Gully. Apart from curving to the left at mid-height, it is identifiable by a huge coffin shaped boulder lying 40m up the bed of the gully.

Approximately 75m further on is Green Gully, easily identified by 'GA' (Grooved Arête) scratched onto the rock 6m to the left of its entrance. It is less pronounced than the previous Gullies and has no continuation beneath the Heather Terrace.

Pinnacle Scramble   Tryfan East Face

Continue up the terrace to reach the 4th significant gully, North Gully. It is narrower and steeper than the previous gullies, with a jammed block forming a cave at 40m up the bed of the gully.

Just beyond the entrance to North Gully, a long, flat-topped boulder sits in the middle of the Heather Terrace, splitting the terrace path. A further 120m along the terrace is the final significant gully, South Gully, which separates South and Central Buttresses. It is identifiable by its broad entrance with a pinnacle standing on the left-hand side. Jammed blocks choke a constriction 30m up the bed of the gully.

Description Start 20m right of South Gully, beneath the most conspicuous of a series of long rock grooves. Enter the groove (easier from the right) and scramble up using excellent holds, at a far more amenable angle than was suggested from below. After 30m, a short detour to the right avoids a smooth section before stepping back into the groove and continuing to a shelf.

Move right for 4m until underneath a huge block, jammed in a groove. Scramble up a cracked rib to the left of the block, to reach a large, sloping platform (first sight of the pinnacle from here). Leave the platform and trend up and right, crossing a series of grooves, then head straight up into a bay. Exit the bay in its upper right hand corner through an obvious slot. Continue directly up over a small rock step and a few easy grooves to reach the pinnacle.

From the rear of the pinnacle, walk right for 15m along a grassy terrace, passing beneath a distinctive v-shaped recess. To the right of the recess is a large perched bollard. Climb up behind the bollard, then scramble up a leftward rising ramp line, to reach a grassy bay situated above the v-shaped recess.

Trend up and left into a groove, following the curving lines created by some unusual thin folds of rock. Pass a very small ledge and continue upwards at a now easier angle, again going with the flow of the rock, to arrive at a narrow ledge. Leave the ledge and scramble easily up the crest of the rib to a large platform beneath the final imposing rock barrier.

Walk around to the right of the barrier and scramble easily up to the summit. A more scenic summit push is to gain the terrace on the left and then contour left under the small roofs, to reach the upper amphitheatre of South Gully (05). A niche in the back wall of the amphitheatre gains the south ridge, which is followed easily to the summit. Descent options are described on page 37.

Emma Twyford following the curious folds of rock that adorn the upper section on **Pinnacle Scramble**

Tania Scotland ambling through the upper narrows of **North Gully**

Scrambling up the easy steps of **Little Gully** into the grand surroundings of **North Gully**

Little and North Gullies

Tryfan East Face

07

Grade	1
Area	Ogwen Valley
Aspect	East (750m)
Approach	50 mins (665 593)

A secluded scramble and the easiest on Tryfan's east face. The route starts up the narrow runnel of Little Gully, which sneaks easily through the impregnable looking base of Central Buttress. It then enters the upper reaches of North Gully, into surroundings that are best described as grand. The rock is solid where it matters and scree is limited to the walking sections. This scramble deserves to be much more popular than it is, receiving a fraction of the visitors compared to the classic North Ridge.

Approach Follow either of the approaches described on page 35 to gain the beginnings of the Heather Terrace, the prominent, wide ramp that runs obliquely across the East Face, rising from north to south.

Head up the terrace path. At first the actual terrace can be difficult to make out, but after a short rise, when the buttresses come into view, the terrace becomes an unmistakable feature; a wide heather and rock covered gangway running up the mountainside.

Cross the first gully, which is little more than a watercourse containing grass and stones, and continue underneath the first proper crags to a better-defined second gully. This is Bastow Gully, which has steep retaining walls and a uniform grassy bed littered with small blocks.

Continue up the terrace for a further 75m to Nor' Nor' Gully. Apart from curving to the left at mid-height, it is identifiable by a huge coffin shaped boulder lying 40m up the bed of the gully.

Approximately 75m further on is Green Gully, easily identified by 'GA' (Grooved Arête) scratched onto the rock 6m to the left of its entrance. It is less pronounced than the previous Gullies and has no continuation beneath the Heather Terrace.

Little and North Gullies   Tryfan East Face

Continue up the terrace to reach the 4th significant gully, North Gully. It is narrower and steeper than the previous gullies, with a jammed block forming a cave at 40m up the bed of the gully.

Just beyond the entrance to North Gully, a long, flat-topped boulder sits in the middle of the Heather Terrace. From 5m beyond this boulder, follow a small subsidiary path up to a recess in the cliff, this is the start of Little Gully.

Description Head up the narrow runnel at the rear of the recess and continue scrambling over a series of short rises to reach a notch at the junction of North Gully.

Walk along a scruffy ledge leading rightwards into the bed of North Gully. A scree-covered path now weaves up the gully bed as it gradually opens out into an impressive upper amphitheatre. Continue to the back of the amphitheatre to reach a terrace supporting the eastern traverse path (see page 65).

There is now a choice of routes. Either head left along the eastern traverse path, which more or less contours around the top of the amphitheatre and literally pops out at the summit. Or, head up the narrow continuation of North Gully, dip under the bridge, and emerge on the North Ridge at the col between the north and main summits. Scramble out of the col and head up the final rise on the North Ridge (12) to arrive directly on the summit. The most commonly used descent routes from Tryfan's summit are described on page 37.

North Buttress Scramble

Tryfan East Face

08

Grade	2-
Area	Ogwen Valley
Aspect	East (710m)
Approach	45 mins (665 594)

A rambling excursion across the broken terrain of North Buttress. Consider it more of a scenic tour rather than an adventurous scramble. The route follows a wandering but logical line through the broken ribs and grassy terraces on the lower part of the buttress. It eventually offers some nice scrambling as it outflanks the impressive Terrace Wall and finishes in a fine position on the North Peak. This is mostly an easy scramble and would warrant a lower grade if not for one 8m high rock step, which is unavoidable.

Approach Follow either of the approaches described on page 35 to gain the beginnings of the Heather Terrace, the prominent, wide ramp that runs obliquely across the East Face, rising from north to south.

Head up the terrace path. At first the actual terrace can be difficult to make out, but after a short rise, when the buttresses come into view, the terrace becomes an unmistakable feature; a wide heather and rock covered gangway running up the mountainside.

Cross the first gully, which is little more than a watercourse containing grass and stones, and continue underneath the first proper crags to a better-defined second gully. This is Bastow Gully, which has steep retaining walls and a uniform grassy bed littered with small blocks.

Continue up the terrace for a further 75m to Nor' Nor' Gully. Apart from curving to the left at mid-height, it is identifiable by a huge coffin shaped boulder lying 40m up the bed of the gully.

Approximately 75m further on is Green Gully, easily identified by 'GA' (Grooved Arête) scratched onto the rock 6m to the left of its entrance. It is less pronounced than the previous gullies and has no continuation beneath the Heather Terrace.

Steve Worth outflanking Terrace Wall on **North Buttress Scramble**

Early morning light on Tryfan's South, Central and North Buttresses

Tryfan East Face — North Buttress Scramble

A further 40m beyond Green Gully is a v-shaped grassy recess with a 3m high flake on its right-hand side. This is the start to North Buttress Scramble.

Description Scramble up the runnel at the back of the recess and after 20m break out right onto a blocky rib. Continue up the rib and its heathery continuation for approximately 30m, to a point just below where the runnel loses its identity.

Cross the runnel and head up a leftward rising ramp line of heather and rock steps. The ramp line traverses underneath a small, clean buttress and leads to an isolated grassy bay at the far left end of the buttress.

Ascend the open corner at the rear of the bay. At just above mid-height on the corner, step up and left onto a ledge on the flat wall. Continue more easily up and left to pop out on an expansive heather and grass terrace. This is the only tricky section on the scramble.

At the rear of the terrace is a continuous slabby rock barrier. Walk over to the far left-hand corner of the terrace to a small recessed corner. Nip up this, then cut horizontally back right for 10m to the foot of a slabby ramp.

Head up the leftward rising ramp, which changes into a rocky groove. This curves back right to reach another grassy terrace - the terrace of Terrace Wall. Standing underneath the impressive Terrace Wall, a continuous, 50m high sheet of rock, it's a no-brainer that the way ahead is not going to be up.

Terrace Wall can be outflanked to the left by following a rocky groove that curves up diagonally beneath the wall. The groove continues as a natural series of steps and short corners, veering back and right into the upper amphitheatre of North Gully.

Continue easily to the gap between North Buttress and the north summit (the eastern traverse path passes through this gap). A short, entertaining scramble, directly out of the gap, leads to the north summit.

From the north summit, a long, rock-strewn saddle connects to a final short scramble up to the main summit. The most commonly used descent routes from Tryfan's summit are described on page 37.

Ben Lawes lurking in the upper reaches of **Nor' Nor' Gully**

Nor' Nor' Grooves

Tryfan East Face

09

Grade	1+
Area	Ogwen Valley
Aspect	East (700m)
Approach	45 mins (665 595)

A pleasant, enclosed scramble through Nor' Nor' Gully, which cleverly avoids the gully's difficult and often wet lower section. Although having far less scrambling than on the popular North Ridge, it is a good alternative giving a quieter and more sheltered route to Tryfan's summit. Worthwhile for its atmosphere and the stark contrast it provides with the more open nature of the North Ridge, which it joins near its top.

Approach Follow either of the approaches described on page 35 to gain the beginnings of the Heather Terrace, the prominent, wide ramp that runs obliquely across the East Face, rising from north to south.

Head up the terrace path. At first the actual terrace can be difficult to make out, but after a short rise, when the buttresses come into view, the terrace becomes an unmistakable feature; a wide heather and rock covered gangway running up the mountainside.

Cross the first gully, which is little more than a watercourse containing grass and stones, and continue underneath the first proper crags to a better-defined second gully. This is Bastow Gully, which has steep retaining walls and a uniform grassy bed littered with small blocks.

Continue up the terrace for a further 75m to Nor' Nor' Gully. Apart from curving to the left at mid-height, it is identifiable by a huge coffin shaped boulder lying 40m up the bed of the gully.

Nor' Nor' Grooves   Tryfan East Face

Description Start by scrambling up a narrow groove on the left retaining wall, just inside the entrance to Nor' Nor' Gully. This is the first in a series of short grooves running slightly above, and parallel with, the main gully. Follow this line of grooves, the last of which leads back into the bed of the gully.

From a recess on the left, scramble up a hidden quartz slab to escape the gully completely. A small track now zig-zags up the open, heathery slope and leads to the right-hand end of a concave rock barrier. Step easily right around the toe of the barrier, back into Nor' Nor' Gully.

Head up the gully, over scree and a few small steps, with the easier line always being to the left. After crossing the eastern traverse path (see page 65), the gully becomes more defined, hemmed in by steep retaining walls. Continue up the atmospheric gully, scrambling past a fallen block forming a bridge, to arrive at the prominent notch on the North Ridge (12).

Escape the Notch by a rightward rising scramble (facing south). Continue along the ridge until the next rise, which contains a steep, block-filled gully. Scramble up the gully, which leads directly to the north summit. A long, rock-strewn saddle then connects to a final scramble up to the main summit. The most commonly used descent routes from Tryfan's summit are described on page 37.

A worthwhile detour is to head straight through the Notch and descend west for 100m, down a rough scree bed, to the base of Notch Arête (633 595), on the true right. The arête is the superb finale of West Face Direct (16) and is arguably the best bit of grade 2 scrambling in North Wales. Once the prominent notch is re-gained, head up the North Ridge to the summit, as described above.

Nor' Nor' Buttress Scramble

Tryfan East Face

10

Grade	3+
Area	Ogwen Valley
Aspect	East (700m)
Approach	45 mins (665 595)

An immensely satisfying scramble, nicely varied and continually challenging from start to finish. The route is a natural line, making a brazen, frontal assault on all the rock features forming the right bounding spur of Nor' Nor' Gully. Expect one or two 'dig deep' moments. A deviation into Nor' Nor' Gully is possible at two thirds height, avoiding a committing technical section and lowering the difficulty by a full grade.

Approach Follow either of the approaches described on page 35 to gain the beginnings of the Heather Terrace, the prominent, wide ramp that runs obliquely across the East Face, rising from north to south.

Head up the terrace path. At first the actual terrace can be difficult to make out, but after a short rise, when the buttresses come into view, the terrace becomes an unmistakable feature; a wide heather and rock covered gangway running up the mountainside.

Cross the first gully, which is little more than a watercourse containing grass and stones, and continue underneath the first proper crags to a better-defined second gully. This is Bastow Gully, which has steep retaining walls and a uniform grassy bed littered with small blocks.

Continue up the terrace for a further 75m to Nor' Nor' Gully. Apart from curving to the left at mid-height, it is identifiable by a huge coffin shaped boulder lying 40m up the bed of the gully.

Description From 5m up Nor' Nor' Gully, ascend a line of heathery steps on the right until underneath a vertical array of blocks at the crest of the buttress. Yard up the hollow sounding blocks to a large grassy platform.

Emma Twyford about to commit to the arête on **Nor' Nor' Buttress Scramble**

Tryfan East Face — Nor' Nor' Buttress Scramble

Rising above the grassy platform is a 20m sweep of clean rock. Climb directly up, using a choice of two wide vertical cracks, to reach another large platform littered with blocks. Situated behind the rocky platform is a solitary perched boulder. Pass behind the boulder, step right, then scramble up a blunt rib on its right-hand side to reach a third platform.

Continue over a few further rock steps and along a broad heather and grass section, to a point where the main bulk of the buttress begins to rear up. From here onwards the buttress is a committing and difficult proposition. If it looks too intimidating on the day, escape leftwards now, into Nor' Nor' Gully*.

Climb up steeply, heading for a large block sitting on a ledge. From the top of the block, step onto the left flank of the sharp arête. Reach onto its crest and ascend delicately to the sanctuary of a triangular grassy platform. An absorbing and exhilarating piece of scrambling.

The next obstacle is the wide, tapering crack, situated directly above and behind the grassy platform. Hidden handholds provide the required security.

Next on the agenda is a 10m high rock scoop, narrowing into a near-vertical corner. Enter the scoop on the right and scramble up to the corner. Exiting the corner is slightly awkward.

Continue easily up a small rib, heading towards the skyline. The grooves to the right of the final narrowing of Nor' Nor' Gully (where it is straddled by a fallen block) provide the most fun way of gaining the North Ridge (12), arriving just to the right of the Notch. Escape the Notch by a rightward rising scramble (facing south). Continue along the ridge until the next rise, which contains a steep, block-filled gully. Scramble up the gully, which leads directly to the north summit. A long, rock-strewn saddle then connects to a final scramble up to the main summit. Descent options are described on page 37.

A worthwhile detour is to descend west from the Notch. Drop down a rough scree bed, for 100m, to the base of Notch Arête (633 595), on the true right. The arête is the superb finale of West Face Direct (16) and is arguably the best bit of grade 2 scrambling in North Wales. Once the prominent notch is re-gained, head up the North Ridge to the summit, as described above.

*If an escape into Nor' Nor' Gully was made, head directly up the gully bed until a vague fork on the right. Surmount a large, slabby boulder by whatever means necessary, then cut back right and enter a hidden, deep cleft. Thrutch up the cleft, regaining the crest of the buttress above the difficult section.

Rob Collister eyeing up the final moves on **Bastow Buttress Scramble**

Bastow Buttress Scramble

Tryfan East Face

11

Grade	2
Area	Ogwen Valley
Aspect	East (660m)
Approach	45 mins (665 595)

A worthwhile route and a good choice as a first foray onto technical scrambling terrain. There are no obligatory hard sections, as an easier alternative (mostly a scree path) runs alongside this route for virtually the whole height of the buttress. Each individual section can simply be taken on or missed out at will. As a bonus, the top of the buttress neatly joins the North Ridge (12) at a point where the best scrambling still remains.

Approach Follow either of the approaches described on page 35 to gain the beginnings of the Heather Terrace, the prominent, wide ramp that runs obliquely across the East Face, rising from north to south.

Head up the terrace path. At first the actual terrace can be difficult to make out, but after a short rise, when the buttresses come into view, the terrace becomes an unmistakable feature; a wide heather and rock covered gangway running up the mountainside.

Cross the first gully, which is little more than a watercourse containing grass and stones, and continue underneath the first proper crags to a better-defined second gully. This is Bastow Gully, which has steep retaining walls and a uniform grassy bed littered with small blocks.

Description From 10m up Bastow Gully, gain the niche on the right and follow a fissure, past a chockstone, to a small ledge on the front of the buttress. Move rightwards in an exposed position, stepping underneath two parallel grooves, to reach a heather ledge. Scramble upwards to reach a much larger heather platform (this same point can also be reached by starting approximately 15m further up Bastow Gully and ascending an easier v-shaped groove).

Bastow Buttress Scramble   Tryfan East Face

A meandering scree path now leads up through easy heather terrain to the next steepening. The steepening, or rise, extends across the width of the buttress.

On the left of the steepening is a wide rock barrier whose left edge overlooks Bastow Gully. An ascent of this barrier is possible but at the upper limit of scrambling technicality. The centre of the steepening comprises a heathery bay capped by blocks, through which the scree path continues. On the right of the steepening is an easy-angled rock rib. Gain the broad crest of this rib and scramble up to the next level section.

When practical, walk left to reach the rocks closest to Bastow Gully. Scramble upwards over ribs and short steps, often in quite exposed positions overlooking the steep wall of the gully. Finally, after a noticeably tricky, small slab, the upper broad crest of Bastow Buttress leads to a large platform on the North Ridge.

The natural continuation from the platform would be to scramble up the remaining, and best part of, the North Ridge (12). Head up the prominent nose of rock at the rear of the platform. The nose is steep and exposed in places, and leads up to a minor summit (the top of Nor' Nor' Buttress).

The scrambling up the nose is excellent; the easiest line starting from a niche behind the spikes at its base. From the minor summit at the top of the nose, carefully down-climb into the Notch.

Escape the Notch by a rightward rising scramble. Continue along the ridge until the next rise, which contains a steep, block-filled gully. Scramble up the gully, which leads directly to the north summit. A long, rock-strewn saddle then connects to a final scramble up to the main summit. Descent options from the summit are described on page 37.

Alternatively, if this is a short outing, head directly down the North Ridge (12) from the platform. Dropping down this lower part of the ridge is not a particularly complicated descent and no prior knowledge of the route is needed. There are numerous well-worn tracks. Head down any of these, staying on the broad crest, until the large heather and boulder covered shoulder is reached approximately 200m above the road. It is then safe to turn to the true left (west) and descend easily down a rough path, beneath the Milestone Buttress. This dog-leg avoids a line of steep ground on the east of the Buttress.

The Eastern Traverse Path is of the special variety and reminiscent of those found among the Cuillin on Skye. It is an intricate but easy to follow route, which weaves across the upper amphitheatres on the east face. The path is a pleasant way of reaching the summit and can be a useful alternative to the final section of the North Ridge (12); it is easier and without exposure, it also is much quieter and offers shelter on blustery days.

The path starts from the large platform on the North Ridge, beneath the steep nose of rock leading to the Notch. Sidle to the left of the nose and follow a wide shelf-line, which leads into the upper amphitheatre of Nor' Nor' Gully. The narrow path then skirts around the amphitheatre, taking a gently-rising line towards a rocky gap, between the north buttress and the north summit.

A scramble over the gap leads into the upper amphitheatre of North Gully. The path then contours around to the far side of the amphitheatre. It then begins to climb, over a series of short scrambly steps, to reach a shoulder on top of the central buttress, directly beneath Adam and Eve.

Standing facing the summit, the path heads left (south), almost into the upper reaches of South Gully, before cutting back up and right. A short scramble then leads to the gap between Adam and Eve.

The **North Ridge of Tryfan** forming the left-hand skyline.

North Ridge

Tryfan

12

Grade	1
Area	Ogwen Valley
Aspect	North (450m)
Approach	20 mins (666 601)

A total classic. If you are only going to do one scramble in North Wales, this is probably the one. Stretching from the valley floor right to the mountain's summit, this beautiful ridge is a landmark for miles around. Good scrambling, solid rock, impressive mountain scenery… it's got the lot. The route isn't particularly difficult in wet or windy conditions; in fact it's an enjoyable adventure in just about any weather.

Approach There are a plenty of parking spots along the stretch of the A5 Ogwen Valley road that runs beneath Tryfan. Rarely, if ever, are they all full. The most direct approach starts by leaving the road from the kissing gate (663 603) at the layby beneath the Milestone Buttress; the prominent buttress on the lower right (west) side of the North Ridge.

Follow the path uphill, staying on the left of the wall, up to the highest stile. The stile is directly beneath the steep crag that runs up and left from the Milestone Buttress. From the stile the path heads left (east), picking its way up to a heather and boulder covered shoulder on the North Ridge. This is the lowest shoulder on the ridge and easily identifiable from the road.

Description The lower part of the ridge is quite broad and offers a number of possible route choices. From a vantage point on the heathery shoulder, choose a weakness in the barrier of steep ground that guards the way ahead. Then head on up. These early stages of the route are literally go-anywhere scrambling, over steep steps of rock interspersed by well-worn tracks.

The best scrambling is found by sticking close to the crest of the ridge or by venturing far over onto the right flank. If in doubt, or in poor visibility, just follow any well-used line. All paths lead to Rome.

North Ridge   Tryfan

The first distinctive feature encountered on the ridge is a large quartz-covered platform. Over to the right (west) of the platform is the Cannon Stone. Boom!

The barrier above the Cannon Stone can be ascended at a number of places. A stepped recess towards its left (east) end gives the most entertaining scrambling and pops out onto another large platform.

At the rear of the platform is a prominent nose of rock. The nose is steep and exposed in places, and leads up to a minor summit (the top of Nor' Nor' Buttress). Head up the nose. The scrambling here is excellent; the easiest line starting from a niche behind the spikes at its base. From the minor summit at the top of the nose, carefully down-climb into the Notch.

The nose can be avoided altogether by following the eastern traverse path (page 65), which is gained by sidling to the left, beneath the blocks forming the base of the nose. Follow the path until underneath a steep-walled gully. Scramble easily up the gully to the Notch.

Escape the Notch by a rightward rising scramble. Continue along the ridge until the next rise, which contains a steep, block-filled gully. Scramble up the gully, which leads directly to the north summit. A long, rock-strewn saddle then connects to a final scramble up to the main summit.

Descents or where next The most commonly used descent routes from Tryfan's summit are described on page 37.

If continuing on a circuit of the Cwm Bochlwyd Horseshoe, head down the South Ridge (17), passing the South Peak on its right (west), to reach a flattening before the rocky protrusion of the Far South Peak. This flattening, or col, is spanned by a stone wall with two stiles (strangely the wall is not shown on any map). Continue south from the flattening, over the Far South Peak, or bypass the peak using a good path to its right (west). Scramble down, trending initially to the true right, then back left, to reach Bwlch Tryfan and the approach to Bristly Ridge (18).

Last of the summer wine - Tony Loxton, George Smith and Mark Lynden on the Cannon Stone

John Redhead on the initial slab of **Milestone Buttress Scramble**

The west flank of Tryfan's Milestone Buttress

Milestone Buttress Scramble

Tryfan West Face

Grade   3
Area   Ogwen Valley
Aspect   West (370m)
Approach   15 mins (663 601)

A tricky little scramble with a few exposed moves. The route takes a rising diagonal line across the Milestone Buttress; the lowest crag on Tryfan's west face, virtually at the foot of the North Ridge. As such, the route makes an exciting approach to the classic North Ridge scramble. The rock is clean and solid but extremely polished. This has no bearing when dry but does make the scramble very slippery in even slightly damp conditions. Be wary of being inquisitive and straying off route, as this is by far the easiest line across the buttress.

Approach There are plenty of parking spots along the A5 Ogwen Valley road that runs beneath Tryfan. Rarely, if ever, are they all full. The most direct approach starts by leaving the road at the kissing gate (663 603) at the lay-by directly beneath the Milestone Buttress.

Follow the path uphill, staying on the left of the wall, as far as the first stile. Cross the wall and trend up and right, across boulders, to the toe of the buttress. Skirt around the buttress, passing beneath its west-facing slabs. To the right and slightly uphill of the main slabs is a solitary narrow slab. Further identified by having two small birch trees clinging to its left side. This protruding narrow slab is the start of the Milestone Scramble

Description Head up the narrow slab using polished but reassuringly deep holds. At half-height, veer left above the birch trees. Continue up the slab to reach a recess below and left of the Pulpit; a distinctive collection of large, flat blocks, stacked on top of each other and jutting out from the crag.

Milestone Buttress   Tryfan West Face

From beneath the Pulpit, head diagonally up and left, following a line of sharp flakes, to reach a small enclosed bay. Exit the bay by swinging out left onto an exposed rippled slab. Continue trending diagonally up and left, across the rippled slab and then across blocks to enter a large walled-in platform.

Escape the platform by scrambling up a spike-filled chimney, located 4m to the right of the platform's rear corner. The chimney is steep but easy, and pops out onto a grassy bay.

Ascend a small groove at the rear right-hand corner of the grassy bay. Above the corner, walk directly uphill over broken ground and large boulders to reach the toe of the continuation buttress; the cleanest and most unbroken area of rock on the hillside. The right-hand (west) side of this buttress takes the form of a small slab, split by a vertical hand-width crack.

Scramble straight up the polished hand-width crack. A dog-leg in the crack is followed by a cheeky step to surmount an overlap. Continue up, over slightly steeper ground, into a vague groove. Good holds at the top of the groove give easy access to a rounded rib, which provides pleasant, easy scrambling until it merges into the hillside.

Descent or where next The easiest descent is to contour left (east) across the hillside, until you intersect with any of the numerous well-worn tracks that cover the lower part of the North Ridge. Head down any of these, staying on the broad crest of the ridge, until the large heather and boulder covered shoulder is reached approximately 200m above the road. It is then safe to turn to the true left (west) and descend easily down a rough path, beneath the Milestone Buttress. This dog-leg avoids a line of steep ground on the east of the Buttress.

To follow on with a scramble up the classic North Ridge (12), continue directly uphill from the top of the Milestone Buttress Scramble. This trajectory hits the broad crest of the ridge at a point just below a large quartz platform, the first distinctive feature encountered during an ascent of the ridge. The most commonly used descent routes from Tryfan's summit are described on page 37.

Milestone Gully

Tryfan West Face

14

Grade	2-
Area	Ogwen Valley
Aspect	West (370m)
Approach	15 mins (663 601)

Entertaining and surprisingly eventful for such a short scramble. The route curls around the back of the Milestone Buttress and ascends a deep, slot-like gully. The rock within the gully is polished and always appears to be wet. In spite of this, it gives over 50m of excellent, sustained scrambling that never feels remotely greasy. Like its neighbour, the Milestone Buttress Scramble (13), this scramble makes a good alternative approach to the classic North Ridge (12), but with only a marginal increase in difficulty.

Approach Walk up to the Milestone Buttress following the description on page 71. Skirt around the buttress, passing beneath its west-facing slabs. To the right of the buttress is a shallow couloir, filled with scree and rock debris. This couloir marks the start of the scramble.

Description Head up the scree-filled couloir, trending left towards its top, to arrive at a platform beneath a black water-washed slab. Scramble up a v-shaped groove to the left of the slab, then curve up and right, behind a cannon stone, to reach a platform.

A chest-high, square-edged shelf bars the way ahead. Hoy yourself over the shelf, or seek a leg-up from a friend.

If the shelf is insurmountable (it's intimidating if on your own), traverse right across a smooth rocky ledge. At the end of the ledge, cut back left and ascend a steep recess to reach a small platform directly beneath the slot-like gully.

Scramble up the cracked left side of the slot-like gully. At its top, exit left over large blocks onto a heather and boulder-covered platform.

Ian Hey ascending the slot-like Milestone Gully

Descents or where next There is no nearby, simple descent back to the foot of the gully. The easiest way down is to take a rising leftward line across the hillside, until you intersect with any of the numerous well-worn tracks that cover the lower part of the North Ridge. Head down any of these, staying on the broad crest of the ridge, until the large heather and boulder covered shoulder is reached at approximately 200m above the road. It is then safe to turn to the true left (west) and descend easily down a rough path, beneath the Milestone Buttress. This dog-leg avoids a line of steep ground on the east of the Buttress.

To follow on with a scramble up the classic North Ridge (12), continue as above, by taking a rising leftward (east) line across the hillside. Then head up any of the well-worn tracks that cover the lower part of the ridge. The most commonly used descent routes from Tryfan's summit are described on page 37.

Alternatively, it is very easy to join the upper section of the Milestone Buttress Scramble (13), at the continuation slab. The foot of which is only 30m from the top of the slot-like gully.

Wrinkled Tower

Tryfan West Face

15

Grade	3
Area	Ogwen Valley
Aspect	West (500m)
Approach	25 mins (662 598)

A short, exciting scramble on excellent rock. Huge, square-cut blocks and smooth walls give this route an unusual and almost architectural quality. It doesn't take much imagination to believe they've been placed with intent rather than arranged by any random force of nature. Its location, low down on Tryfan's west face, makes the route an ideal choice for a quick outing (especially good in the latter part of a sunny day). There is also little time penalty if the route is chosen as a spicier start to the classic North Ridge.

Approach There are plenty of parking spots along the stretch of the A5 Ogwen Valley road running beneath Tryfan. Rarely, if ever, are they all full. The most practical approach starts slightly west of Tryfan, leaving the road at the kissing gate (661 603), opposite the crescent shaped lay-by. This approach is not the quickest but allows you to scope out the layout of the West Face.

From the kissing gate, follow a vague grassy track, which zig-zags steeply up the hillside (it can be obscured by bracken from late summer onwards). Initially the track sticks to a rough distance of 125m from the West Face, enough to give an unrestricted view of all the features on the face.

The lower slopes of the face consist mainly of heather-covered slabs and discontinuous rocky ribs. Approximately 225m from the Milestone Buttress, along the bottom of the face, is an area of continuous rock slabs. To the right of these slabs is a wide scree-filled couloir. Wrinkled Tower starts at the entrance to this couloir and follows the rocky rib bounding its left-hand side.

Description Start at the entrance of the couloir, where the lowest in a series of slabs touches the scree. Take a rising leftward line across the easy-angled slabs to reach a bay beneath the angular cornered walls of the buttress.

Martyn Eade on a summer's evening scramble over the Wrinkled Tower

Tryfan West Face **Wrinkled Tower**

From the bay, scramble up over rough, pockmarked slabs to reach a headwall and then scramble left onto a grassy platform piled with rocks. Above the platform is a nose of rock containing a niche. Climb easily into the niche, then continue in a 10 o'clock direction, using a perfectly positioned, leftward sloping flake, to gain the blocky crest of the Buttress.

Scramble upwards over huge blocks, bypassing two large pinnacles on their right. Continue along the crest of the buttress, which quickly changes into a gently-angled broad rib. Stop at the end of the rib when level with the base of an imposing rock tower.

At the end of the rib, cross a grassy depression and gain the quartz platform at the base of the tower. The next section is decidedly tricky and serious. Thrutch up the chimney that splits the tower, passing an awkward jammed flake on the way. From the sanctuary of the wide upper chimney, inch out leftwards along a sloping ramp, onto the face of the tower. An excellent hold on the extreme left edge facilitates a heart-stopping move up onto a flat ledge. Phew!

If all this sounds too much, the chimney and face can easily be avoided by sidling left around the tower, then scrambling back right to gain the flat ledge at the top of the difficulties.

Gain the crest of the tower by either climbing directly above the ledge or by skirting left to enter a deep cleft, where some strenuous moves bring you out on top. Walk 10m uphill to the base of a beautiful slab, split by a vertical crack. Cruise up the crack and continue along a vague, intermittent rock rib to reach the North Ridge, at a point just above the Cannon Stone.

Descent or Where Next The quickest and easiest descent is to head down any of the numerous well-worn tracks that cover the lower part of the North Ridge. Stay on the broad crest of the ridge until the large heather and boulder covered shoulder is reached at approximately 200m above the road. It is then safe to turn to the true left (west) and descend easily down a rough path, beneath the Milestone Buttress. This dog-leg avoids a line of steep ground on the east of the Buttress.

The natural continuation to Wrinkled Tower would be to head up the North Ridge (12). Especially as the best of the ridge's scrambling is still to come and over half the mountain's height has already been climbed. The most commonly used descent routes from Tryfan's summit are described on page 37.

Aaron Harris starting an evening ascent of the superb **Notch Arête**

George Smith properly gripped on the crux of **Wrinkled Tower**

West Face Direct

Tryfan West Face

16

Grade	2+
Area	Ogwen Valley
Aspect	West (650m)
Approach	40 mins (662 595)

A **'must do' scramble** following a natural line up the centre of this often neglected face. The lower half of the route is perhaps more of a scenic ramble through the boulder-choked fault line of Y Gully. However, short diversions onto the excellent rock of the gully's left wall provide more than enough scrambling interest. The upper half of the route, along the crest of Notch Arête, is probably the best quality scrambling of its grade in North Wales, with a position that is simply lovely. Catches the afternoon sun throughout the year and well into the late evening during the summer.

Approach There are plenty of parking spots along the stretch of the A5 Ogwen Valley road running beneath Tryfan. Rarely, if ever, are they all full. The most practical approach starts slightly west of Tryfan, leaving the road at the kissing gate (661 603), opposite the crescent shaped lay-by.

From the kissing gate, follow a vague grassy track, which zig-zags steeply up the hillside (it can be hidden by bracken from late summer onwards). Initially the track sticks to a rough distance of 125m from the West Face, enough to give an unrestricted view of all the features on the face. Continue up the track, which becomes increasingly faint as height is gained. It weaves up the right bank of a watercourse on the upper part of the hillside, before slowly veering towards the face.

Looking up towards the right (south) side of the face, there are two very distinctive gullies. The first gully, called V Cleft, is deep and fan-shaped, with an arête bounding each side. The second gully, further up the hillside, curves up to the right. As you approach this second gully, called Y Gully, a left branch appears. This left branch is unmistakable. It is perfectly straight, runs directly up the hillside and is choked with huge boulders. It is the start of the scramble.

Mark Lynden on a summer afternoon's ascent of **Notch Arête** on **West Face Direct**

The West Face of Tryfan

Tryfan West Face — **West Face Direct**

Description Enter the gully on the left, passing the first jammed blocks on the right. The second set of jammed blocks can be passed either on the right by a short chimney, or more easily on the left via some clean slabby steps. Continue up the gully towards the final constriction of jumbled blocks and pop into the hole on the right-hand side (mandatory of course) emerging easily onto their top.

From the top of the jumbled blocks ascend the left bounding wall of the gully and tip toe up the beautiful cracked arête. A second, more delicate arête follows soon afterwards, again forming the left bounding wall of the gully.

From the top of the arête, sidle left across the hillside onto jumbled blocks and continue upwards. From the top of these blocks, trend slightly left for 50m, across almost level ground, to the base of Notch Arête; a small truncating buttress with a detached, 8m high, pointed obelisk at its centre.

A stepped corner at the right toe of the buttress (directly under a perched block) gives access to a large platform. A direct ascent of the barrier behind the platform is too difficult. Instead, go to the far left of the platform and locate a deep fissure, just around a corner. Squirm up the fissure with enormous difficulty, exiting obliquely right, through a niche, to gain the crest of the arête. If the squirming fails, skulk up the scree couloir on the right of the arête and clamber onto the crest at the first easy opportunity.

Exquisite scrambling, over crack slabs and smooth ribs, leads up to the North Ridge, arriving just before the prominent notch on its skyline.

Descent or Where Next Drop into the Notch then escape by a rightward rising scramble (facing south). Continue along the North Ridge (12) until the next rise, which contains a steep, block-filled gully. Scramble up the gully, which leads directly to the north summit. A long, rock-strewn saddle then connects to a final scramble up to the main summit. The most commonly used descent routes from Tryfan's summit are described on page 37.

Matt Hawkins and Aaron Harris scrambling in **Y Gully** on Tryfan's **West Face Direct**

South Ridge

Tryfan

17

Grade	1-
Area	Ogwen Valley
Aspect	South (820m)
Approach	70 mins (663 592)

A gentle scramble and the easiest on Tryfan. The route picks an arbitrary line up the broad crest of the mountain's South Ridge. Difficulties can be taken on at will or avoided altogether. Good fun, always manageable and finishing on a magnificent rocky summit. An ideal outing for kids to experience their first 'hands on' ascent of a mountain, as countless school groups have done for decades.

Approach From the Visitor Centre at Ogwen Cottage, follow the path that runs up and left from the entrance to the old slate cutting. After a few hundred metres the main path curves back right towards Llyn Idwal. At this point, head diagonally leftwards on the smaller Cwm Bochlwyd path, which eventually climbs steeply up the side of a cascading stream to reach the outflow of Llyn Bochlwyd. More direct approaches are possible from any of the parking areas further along the A5 Ogwen Valley road towards Tryfan.

From the outflow of Llyn Bochlwyd, follow the good path on the left side of the lake. After 150m the path heads obliquely up the hillside to Bwlch Tryfan; the lowest point between Tryfan and Glyder Fach.

From Bwlch Tryfan, head north, staying to the left of the wall. Skirt around the Far South Peak on its left flank, or scramble over its top, to reach a flattening beneath the South Ridge. This flattening, or col, is spanned by a stone wall with two stiles. The wall is not shown on any map.

Description The South Summit can be ascended by a scrambly path, which starts slightly to the left (west) of the flattening and takes an easy-to-follow line through nice, rocky scenery.

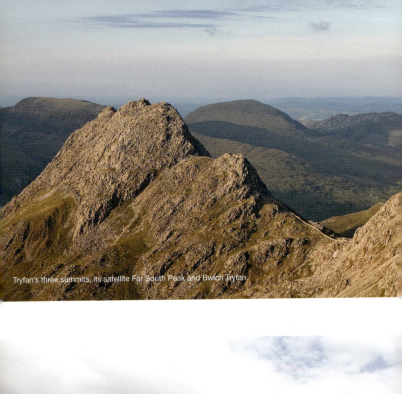

Tryfan's three summits, its satellite Far South Peak and Bwlch Tryfan

Path

17

Tryfan's South Summit on the approach from Bwlch Tryfan

Tryfan **South Ridge**

Anywhere to the right of path, on the broad crest of the ridge, gives good, fun, straightforward scrambling. Comprising short rock steps punctuated by large ledges. The scrambling is escapable at any point, by simply heading back over to the path.

From the South Summit, cross a broad rocky saddle to reach Tryfan's Central Summit and the twin standing stones of Adam and Eve.

Descent or where next The quickest descent from Tryfan's summit is via the west flank route, described on page 37. Bear in mind that this is a marginally more difficult option than going back down the South Ridge.

Streaky Desroy at one with the world on Glyder Fach's main cliff

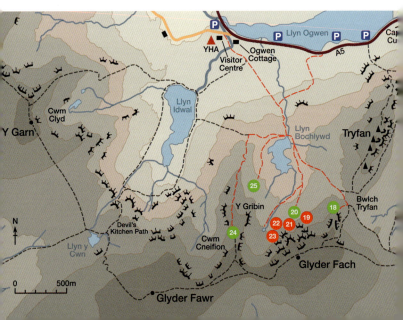

Glyder Fach Main Cliff

Ogwen Valley

18	Bristly Ridge	1
19	Chasm Face Route	3+
20	Main Gully	1+
21	East Gully Ridge	3+
22	Hawks Nest Buttress Scramble	3+
23	Dolmen Ridge	3

Glyder Fach (994m) and Glyder Fawr (1001m) are the two highest mountains in the Glyders (Glyderau in Welsh) and are located at the eastern end of the range, on the south side of the Ogwen Valley. They are most well known for their extensive and unusual summit plateaus, which are connected by a broad grassy ridge. The edge of this plateau area, along its northern aspects, drops off into a number of high-mountain cwms. The steep cliffs of these cwms, and their dividing ridges, create a climbing and scrambling playground.

Cwm Bochlwyd is located directly beneath the summit of Glyder Fach. At the head of the cwm is Glyder Fach's Main Cliff. It is here that you'll find an exceptionally high concentration of good quality scrambles. In fact, from purely a technical perspective, this is some of the best scrambling in Britain.

The main cliff of Glyder Fach isn't a cliff in the true sense of mountaineering terminology. It's more a chaotic sprawl of buttresses and rock bands on the mountain's steep northwest slopes. Within this sprawl are three main buttresses, each being the truncated end to a well-defined ridge running down from the summit plateau. These ridges are difficult to distinguish on approach and only reveal themselves as height is gained or when the afternoon sun casts their shadow.

The cliff is worth a visit at any time of year and always provides an abundance of high mountain ambience. In summer, when it receives afternoon and evening sun, there are few finer places to go scrambling. In midwinter the cliff is completely devoid of any warming sunlight and can feel a quite inhospitable place, particularly in strong north or northwesterly winds. Bear this in mind when thinking of a winter visit, give extra consideration to wind direction and avoid an elemental suffer-fest.

Lou Lawrence and Kat Dunbar pause on the Cantilever Stone

Glyder Fach Main Cliff

In general, the rock on the main cliff is clean, ubiquitously solid and a pure joy to move across. On the buttresses, where the rock is compact and steep, the nature of the scrambling is committing and often requires some precision route finding. In contrast, on the upper slopes and ridges, where the rock is interspersed by terraces, the scrambling is open to variation and beckons for an exploratory approach.

The cliff dries quickly after any rain and surprisingly isn't vulnerable to drainage from the upper slopes. Greasy rock can occasionally be present on the lower buttress sections but this is never an issue after a few days of dry weather. It's not an unreasonable proposition to tackle any of the selected scrambles in the wet, though be warned the excitement level on the harder routes is likely to become highly amped ...or as it was phrased in guidebooks of old, 'the grade may be augmented somewhat'.

Glyder Fach's summit plateau has an otherworldly feel. It belongs more to the pages of a fantasy tale than to a natural landscape. Dotted around the plateau are huge piles of jumbled plinths. The random arrangement of each pile has an unearthly hint of intention. None more so than the pile containing the Cantilever Stone; the long, carefully balanced plank of rock, which calls out to be walked along.

The most dramatic of the plateau's features is Castell y Gwynt (Castle of the Wind). The massive structure of upturned plinths is located 300m southwest of the summit and as its name suggests, could, from a distance, be easily mistaken for a long-abandoned fortification.

Approach to the Main Cliff From the Visitor Centre at Ogwen Cottage, follow the path that runs up and left from the entrance to the old slate cutting. After a few hundred metres the main path curves back right towards Llyn Idwal. At this point, head diagonally left (southeast) on the smaller Cwm Bochlwyd path, which eventually climbs steeply up the side of a cascading stream to reach the outflow of Llyn Bochlwyd. More direct approaches are possible from any of the parking areas further along the A5 Ogwen Valley road towards Tryfan.

From the stream outflow, skirt leftwards around the lake. There is a faint but discernible track undulating between 10 and 20 metres above the shoreline, which will help keep your feet dry. At the far end of the lake numerous small tracks lead up easily through the scree slope to the base of the main cliff.

Glyder Fach Main Cliff

Lou Lawrence on an early morning dash up the classic **Bristly Ridge**

Bristly Ridge

Glyder Fach Main Cliff

18

Grade	1
Area	Ogwen Valley
Aspect	Northwest (800m)
Approach	60 mins (661 587)

Famous and justifiably so; perhaps the embodiment of North Wales scrambling. Seen in profile, the ridge's pinnacled crest takes on a fairytale form. It is beautiful yet looks impossible; two qualities that make it a compelling mountaineering line. The scrambling is far easier than appearance would suggest. The rock is littered with huge holds and despite being polished is not especially slippery when wet. To be savoured ahead of the masses on an early morning ascent.

Approach Follow the approach route from the Ogwen Valley to Cwm Bochlwyd, described on page 89. The distinctive pinnacled outline of Bristly Ridge comes into view as you reach the Cwm. It defines the left edge of Glyder Fach's main cliff, dropping down from the summit plateau to Bwlch Tryfan; the lowest point between Tryfan and Glyder Fach.

From the outflow of Llyn Bochlwyd, follow the good path on the left side of the lake. After 150m the path heads obliquely up the hillside towards Bwlch Tryfan.

From the Bwlch, follow the stone wall (southwest) to the foot of the lowest rocks forming the base of Bristly Ridge. At the wall's end, skirt rightwards beneath the rocks for 10m and ascend a short gully, exiting left to arrive at a small, incongruous man-made wall.

Behind the small stone wall is the entrance to a hidden, well-defined gully, often referred to as Sinister Gully. Contrary to its name this gully is the safest and most aesthetic way of gaining the crest of Bristly Ridge. It is important to make sure you have correctly identified the gully, which can be confirmed by looking for a large jutting prow of rock that overhangs the gully's narrow confines mid-way up. There are two other similar sized gullies, both of which have become perilously eroded at their exits resulting in stonefall danger.

The distinctive pinnacled crest of **Bristly Ridge**

Description Scramble carefully up the enclosed gully bed, avoiding a steep section at half height (underneath the jutting prow) by veering onto the left wall of the gully. Approximately 10m before the head of the gully, exit on the left by a gently rising, quartz-paved ramp to reach the broad crest of the ridge.

Continue easily up the ridge by a variety of possible lines, the best and most exhilarating being as close to the crest as possible. After a slabby shoulder, the ridge narrows and rises up to reach a rocky turret lying transverse to the direction of the ridge.

Climb over the turret and descend leftwards into the atmospheric Great Pinnacle Gap. Go through the gap and escape over a 2m step to the right of the elegant 10m high Pinnacle. Regain the crest of the ridge by scrambling leftwards up a groove system or tackle a steeper wall slightly to the right. Continue more easily along the superb ridge (avoiding an easier path on the right) to the summit plateau.

Glyder Fach Main Cliff **Bristly Ridge**

Descents or where next A vague but frequently cairned path crosses the rocky summit plateau to Glyder Fach's summit mound, which is 300m away, to the southwest. The path passes close to the jumble of plinths containing the Cantilever Stone. The circuit of the Cwm Bochlwyd Horseshoe continues with a descent of Y Gribin, described below.

The following **descent options from Glyder Fach** are described from the summit and are applicable for all the Main Cliff scrambles. The quickest descent route is to head northeast from the summit mound, along a frequently cairned path. Where the path veers to the east, continue northeast, dropping down slightly, to reach a large cairn on the immediate true right of the pronounced top of Bristly Ridge.

The large cairn marks the top of a rubble and scree slope, which runs down the east side of Bristly Ridge to Bwlch Tryfan. The slope is well-used and severely eroded. Consequently there is a real risk of being hit by stones dislodged by other parties. Stay well over to the true right whilst descending, which will keep you out of the fall line.

A more pleasant and less nerve wracking descent also heads northeast along the cairned path. Stay on the path as it veers east before dropping down the southeast shoulder of the mountain. Stop 200m short of Llyn Caseg-fraith, then cut sharply back left to follow the well-established Miner's Track, which contours across the hillside to Bwlch Tryfan.

A descent is also possible on the western side of the mountain, down Y Gribin (24); the long ridge separating Cwm Bochlwyd from Cwm Cneifion. Head southwest from the summit mound to the unmistakable rock feature of Castell y Gwynt. Scramble through the Castell's jumbled plinths and drop into Bwlch y Ddwy-Glyder. From the Bwlch, take the upper of two paths, which hugs the cliff edge overlooking Cwm Bochlwyd, and follow it to a large cairn at the top of the promontory.

The cairn marks the top of Y Gribin. For a scrambly descent, head straight down the crest of the narrow, upper rock rib. To avoid all difficulties, take the rough, zig-zag scree path on the true left of the rib. From the base of the rib, descend northwest, down a scree path, to reach the large grassy plateau, known locally as 'the Football Field'. Cross to the northern end of the grassy field, from where a good path, on the true right flank of the lower ridge, leads to the outflow of Llyn Bochlwyd. The paved path used on the approach can then be followed back to the Ogwen Valley road.

Streaky Desroy creeping up the infamous Cat-walk on **Chasm Face Route**

Chasm Face Route

Glyder Fach Main Cliff

19

Grade	3+
Area	Ogwen Valley
Aspect	Northwest (800m)
Approach	60 mins (656 586)

A hard, burly scramble where good mountaineering nous and a forceful approach are essential, especially if tackled in wet conditions. The lower section is continuously challenging and sneaks deviously through the Chasm Face, the steep truncating cliff of East Buttress. In contrast, the upper section is relatively straightforward, involving pleasant, open scrambling on superb rock with no surprises. All in all, a top class excursion.

Approach Follow the approach route from the Ogwen Valley to the base of the Main Cliff, which is described on page 89.

The scramble starts up a vague depression, just to the left of Alphabet Slab – the obvious smooth triangular band of rock situated below and slightly right of the East Buttress. In poor visibility, the slab is identified by being the continuous stretch of rock that is furthermost left (east) along the base of the cliff, above the scree slopes. If you continue too far left, beyond the Alphabet Slab, the base of the cliff immediately becomes broken and poorly defined.

Description Starting from a few metres left of Alphabet Slab, head up the depression that takes a rightward-rising line to the rear of the slab. Easy scrambling for 120m reaches a narrowing blocked by a chockstone. Climb past the chockstone to access a large area of grassy ledges. This requires a surprising degree of confident bridging.

Head immediately left, passing over the Chasm itself (a deep square cut fissure), and heave awkwardly over piled blocks to gain a triangular bay below a smooth, impossible looking corner.

Chasm Face Route   Glyder Fach Main Cliff

Climb upwards for 3m just to the left of the corner. Then move bravely leftwards onto the steep wall to follow a series of positive flakes (protectable) to reach the sanctuary of a significant notch after a further 6m.

Ahead lies the infamous 'Cat-Walk', a half metre wide ramp line leading to an upper bay spanned by a huge fallen block. Creep up the Cat-Walk (exposed but not too difficult) and scramble up to a point beneath the fallen block, negotiating a tricky step on the way (this can be the crux if wet).

The route now splits. Tubsters and claustrophobics can mount the fallen block and escape rightwards, taking an enjoyable detour through the central section of 'Main Gully'. Masochists can continue to the upper left corner of the bay and enter the depths of Glyder Fach via an unlikely narrow cleft.

Breathe in deeply and squirm through the cleft to arrive at a thankfully wider, vertical chimney. This leads, via some nifty back and footing, to daylight and the crest of East Buttress. The main difficulties are now over and the route continues delightfully over the blocky outcrops that litter the upper slope before reaching the summit plateau.

Descents or where next The quickest way back to the base of the Main Cliff is down the adjacent Main Gully (20). The gully's upper bowl is a little scrappy and requires care. At a junction near the bottom of the bowl, veer to the true right, staying close beneath the Chasm Face. Do not descend East Gully.

The most interesting descent by far is down the superb Bristly Ridge (18). The protruding crest of the ridge is located at the eastern end of the Main Cliff. Descending the ridge is surprisingly uncomplicated. However, make sure you correctly identify Sinister Gully near the base of the ridge. A jutting prow half-way down and a gully top not threatened by loose rock and debris are the giveaways.

The most commonly used descent routes from Glyder Fach's summit are described on page 95.

Main Gully

Glyder Fach Main Cliff

20

Grade	1+
Area	Ogwen Valley
Aspect	Northwest (800m)
Approach	60 mins (656 586)

An atmospheric route that curves up beneath the steep walls and pillars of the East Buttress before taking a more open line direct to the summit plateau. There is only one problematic short step in this otherwise straightforward gully, which passes through terrain normally reserved for rock climbs and harder scrambles. It is a surprisingly good scramble; an extremely scenic and quiet route to the summit of Glyder Fach.

Approach Follow the approach route from the Ogwen Valley to the base of the Main Cliff, which is described on page 89.

The scramble starts up a vague depression, just to the left of Alphabet Slab – the obvious smooth triangular band of rock situated below and slightly right of the East Buttress. In poor visibility, the slab is identified by being the continuous stretch of rock that is furthermost left (east) along the base of the cliff, above the scree slopes. If you continue too far left, beyond the Alphabet Slab, the base of the cliff immediately becomes broken and poorly defined.

Description Starting from a few metres left of Alphabet Slab, head up the depression that takes a rightward-rising line to the rear of the slab. Easy scrambling for 120m reaches a narrowing blocked by a chockstone. Getting past the chockstone is rather awkward and requires either confident bridging technique or even a helpful 'leg up' from a partner.

Continue up the wide, easy-angled depression, passing beneath the towering columns of the Chasm Face to the left and the smooth confining rock walls to the right.

Main Gully   Glyder Fach Main Cliff

After 50m the gully begins to steepen and you will be naturally channelled towards a slot-like constriction. Climb the outside of the slot. It is steep but with an abundance of good holds. The steepness soon eases off and the gully once again opens up to a series of grassy ledges.

At the first available opportunity, trend left to gain the top of the Chasm Face and the broad crest of East Buttress. From here, delightful scrambling over short blocky outcrops leads directly to the summit plateau.

Descents or where next If you found scrambling up Main Gully to be okay, a descent of the superb Bristly Ridge (18) should be within your ability. The two scrambles complement each other well in a round trip to Glyder Fach's summit. The protruding crest of the Bristly Ridge is located at the eastern end of the Main Cliff. Descending the ridge is surprisingly uncomplicated. However, make sure you correctly identify Sinister Gully near the base of the ridge. A jutting prow half-way down, and a gully top not threatened by loose rock and debris are the giveaways.

The most commonly used descent routes from Glyder Fach's summit are described on page 95.

Paul Dickson bridging past the awkward chockstone in **Main Gully**

Libby Peter on the superb central section of **East Gully Ridge**

East Gully Ridge

Glyder Fach Main Cliff

21

Grade	3+
Area	Ogwen Valley
Aspect	Northwest (800m)
Approach	60 mins (655 584)

A technically challenging route at the upper end of the scrambling spectrum. Some teams may wish to employ pitched rock climbing tactics to surmount one or more of the intimidating sections. Despite this, it is not a committing scramble and an escape, or an easier detour, is possible at just about every point apart from the initial 40m. It takes a direct, well-defined line overlooking East Gully and has a good mountaineering feel to it.

Approach Follow the approach route from the Ogwen Valley to the base of the Main Cliff, which is described on page 89.

The scramble starts at the entrance to East Gully. This is the prominent deep slot situated almost centrally, and at the lowest point, in the entire main cliff. In poor visibility it can be located approximately 75m to the right of the more easily recognizable Alphabet slab - the smooth triangular band of rock that is furthermost left (east) along the base of the cliff, above the scree slopes. Go left too far, beyond the Alphabet Slab, and the base of the cliff immediately becomes broken and poorly defined.

Description Clamber into the gully to reach a spacious bay beneath a point where the gully steepens and becomes more of a dank chimney. Climb leftwards out of the bay following the quartz seam, which leads steeply to a platform with a handy belay spike at 15m.

Step out right from the spike and ascend the disconcertingly steep, slabby rock, weaving around to find the line of least resistance, to eventually arrive at a large terrace after 25m.

East Gully Ridge   Glyder Fach Main Cliff

An impregnable 4m wall now blocks the way ahead. From the right hand end of the terrace, outflank the wall by initially scrambling up right, then back left. Easier ground now leads to the base of a rocky rib.

The rib is in a fine position overlooking East Gully. Ascend the large steps on its crest to arrive at a platform behind a jumble of blocks. At the rear of the platform the rib rises abruptly, with only an ominous 2m vertical crack offering any hope of progress.

Climb precariously up the vertical crack and position yourself on a small ledge. Now make a hard, insecure move up and left, on virtual footholds, to a flattening on the crest of the rib. If all this looks far too daunting, don't start climbing the vertical crack (difficult to reverse). Instead, from the base of the rise, skirt around to the right and ascend an easy 2m slab, from where an energetic but far more secure move gains a niche high on the left. This in turn gives access to the flattening on the crest of the rib.

Continue more easily up the well-defined ridge on good, solid rock. The ridge gradually loses definition, veering left across the top of Main Gully, to merge into the blocky outcrops on the broad crest of East Buttress. Delightful, trouble-free scrambling leads to the summit plateau.

Descents or where next The quickest way back to the base of the Main Cliff is down the adjacent Main Gully (20). The gully's upper bowl is a little scrappy and requires care. At a junction near the bottom of the bowl, veer to the true right, staying close beneath the Chasm Face. Do not descend East Gully.

The most interesting descent by far is down the superb Bristly Ridge (18). The protruding crest of the ridge is located at the eastern end of the Main Cliff. Descending the ridge is surprisingly uncomplicated. However, make sure you correctly identify Sinister Gully near the base of the ridge. A jutting prow half-way down, and a gully top not threatened by loose rock and debris are the giveaways.

The most commonly used descent routes from Glyder Fach's summit are described on page 95.

Hawks Nest Buttress Scramble

Glyder Fach Main Cliff

22

Grade	3+
Area	Ogwen Valley
Aspect	Northwest (800m)
Approach	60 mins (655 584)

An absolute belter of a scramble. It is technically hard, with a heady mix of both thuggish and delicate sections. It is the longest scramble on the main cliff and is continuously interesting from start to finish. The central section is particularly committing and would be very difficult to reverse without a rope. The upper slopes are open to variation and offer superb exploratory scrambling on generally good rock.

Approach Follow the approach route from the Ogwen Valley to the base of the Main Cliff, which is described on page 89.

The scramble starts beneath Hawks Nest Buttress, at a point approximately 50m right of the entrance to East Gully. This is the prominent deep slot situated almost centrally, and at the lowest point, in the entire Main Cliff.

Description Scramble up easy broken terrain, trending left to reach a large grassy shoulder. This sits directly beneath Hawk's Nest Buttress, a compact vertical tower with a broad rippled slab fanning out at its base.

Climb diagonally right across the slabs (intimidating but not difficult) to a recess at the right-hand edge of the buttress. Further right again is an obvious notch behind a large pinnacle, which is reached by an intimidating, exposed shuffle along a narrow ledge.

From the comfort of the notch, make a tricky move up a smooth, slabby wall to gain a large enclosed bay. Continue directly ahead up a grassy depression, which funnels into the confines of a rocky groove in the upper left corner of the bay.

Mark Lynden escaping the bite of the shark on **Hawks Nest Buttress Scramble**

Glyder Fach Main Cliff — **Hawks Nest Buttress**

Once in the seemingly inescapable groove, look above your left shoulder to see an angular niche capped by a 1m prow of rock. This is where the scramble goes next. Climb into the niche, and then using the prow and whatever simian technique comes to hand, pull onto the platform at the front of the buttress. You are now committed and past the point of no return.

A huge pinnacle overlooks the platform, with a jammed chockstone at its top. To its right is a smooth cornered recess. Clamber over jumbled blocks to reach the base of the smooth corner and with the aid of a wide crack, gain a small spike at 3m. From the top of the spike, a wild step left (protectable) onto the crest of the left wall, followed by a short slab, leads thankfully to some block belays.

Rising up ahead is Shark Pinnacle. It's actually two pinnacles with the uncanny resemblance of a feeding shark. The photographic opportunity of standing between the shark's jaws is a rite of passage.

Behind Shark Pinnacle is a small rock barrier. This can be ascended on the left by a short corner. Excellent easier scrambling now follows, with a number of possible lines penetrating the blocky outcrops on the broad crest of the buttress before joining the upper part of Dolmen Ridge. This is exploratory scrambling at its best.

Descents or where next The quickest way back to the base of the Main Cliff is down the adjacent Main Gully (20). The gully's upper bowl is a little scrappy and requires care. At the bottom of the bowl, veer to the true right, staying close beneath the Chasm Face. Do not descend East Gully.

The most interesting descent by far is down the superb Bristly Ridge (18). The protruding crest of the ridge is located at the eastern end of the Main Cliff. Descending the ridge is surprisingly uncomplicated. However, make sure you correctly identify Sinister Gully near the base of the ridge. A jutting prow half-way down, and a gully top not threatened by loose rock and debris are the giveaways.

The most commonly used descent routes from Glyder Fach's summit are described on page 95.

Streaky Desroy entering the steep corner leading to the crest of the **Dolmen Ridge**

Dolmen Ridge

Glyder Fach Main Cliff

23

Grade	3
Area	Ogwen Valley
Aspect	Northwest (800m)
Approach	70 mins (654 585)

An outstanding route that meanders through impressive mountain terrain without ever being unduly difficult. The exact line of this scramble is complex but never too tricky to follow, with helpful navigational features littered along the way. Even when tackled in mist and drizzle it is a brilliant Tolkien-esque journey. The main difficulty may be stopping your imagination running riot. Arguably the best grade 3 outing in the Ogwen Valley.

Approach Follow the approach route from the Ogwen Valley to Cwm Bochlwyd, which is described on page 89.

From the outflow of Llyn Bochlwyd, skirt leftwards around the lake. There is a faint but discernible track undulating between 10 and 20 metres above the shoreline, which will help keep your feet dry. At the far end of the lake allow yourself to be funnelled up the main watercourse to a small pool (653 585) in the far back right of the cwm.

From the pool, head across to the base of West Gully; the long depression running down the right-hand side of the main cliff, narrowing towards its base and with a broad scree fan beneath it. In poor visibility, a southeasterly bearing will take you directly to its entrance.

The scramble begins at the toe of the quartz-marked rocks that form the left bounding wall of West Gully.

Description Scramble up and left over the tiers of quartz-marked rock and grassy ledges, to eventually reach one of two grassy bays. On first impression the bays seem inescapable; they are connected by a narrow grassy gangway but hemmed in by 4m walls in every direction.

Dolmen Ridge   Glyder Fach Main Cliff

Passage to the next level is unlocked by a very sneaky step, hidden behind the two distinct rock pinnacles that overlook the left-hand bay. Climb onto a platform directly beneath the twin pinnacles. Now commit to a heart-stopping heave, using good incut holds, to gain a sloping platform and access to 'the courtyard'; a sloping, quartz-paved area below the fortress-like Dolmen Buttress.

Cross 'the courtyard' to the far right-hand corner of the Buttress. Turn the corner, step across the gully, and then move horizontally right for 5m before clambering up to regain the now wider gully bed.

Walk 30m up the stone-strewn gully until level with a ramp-line that leads back leftwards, to the front of the buttress. Spectacular.

From the end of the ramp, climb into a niche and ascend a steep corner system, using positive holds, to reach the crest of the main ridge. A superb, airy section with an aura more of the high mountains than that normally felt in North Wales.

Follow the crest of the ridge, with consistently interesting scrambling, to reach the Dolmen block (a flat-topped jumble of boulders resembling an ancient burial chamber). Further flat-topped obstacles follow on and can all be tackled direct, the final one being avoidable on the left if necessary.

The ridge now eases and curves majestically up to the right, eventually merging into the main bulk of the mountain after passing the top of west gully. Easy scrambling now leads up through the summit slopes.

Descents or where next An alternative way back to the base of the Dolmen Ridge is to bail down from Bwlch y Ddwy-Glyder; the col located at the western end of the Main Cliff, just beyond Castell y Gwynt. When descending, veer to the true right, beneath the north cliffs of the Castell.

The most interesting descent by far is down the superb Bristly Ridge (18). The protruding crest of the ridge is located at the eastern end of the Main Cliff. Descending the ridge is surprisingly uncomplicated. However, make sure you correctly identify Sinister Gully near the base of the ridge. A jutting prow half-way down and a gully top not threatened by loose rock and debris are the giveaways. The most commonly used descent routes from Glyder Fach's summit are described on page 95.

Libby Peter unlocking the way to 'the courtyard' on the lower section of the **Dolmen Ridge**

Tania Scotland crossing the Football Field en route to the prominent rock rib on **Y Gribin**

Y Gribin

Glyder Fawr

24

Grade	1
Area	Ogwen Valley
Aspect	North (830m)
Approach	60 mins (651 585)

An impressive and easy scramble, which ascends the crest of a fine rocky rib. It may be short and always escapable, but the situations are great and it never feels contrived. The scrambling isn't bad either. The rib is located at the top of Y Gribin, the broad spur separating Cwm Bochlwyd and Cwm Cneifion. It rises up midway between Glyder Fach and Glyder Fawr, to arrive at the grassy ridge that connects their summit plateaus. The path to the rib's side is a very popular route up, and down, either of these mountains.

Approach Follow the approach described on page 89 to reach Llyn Bochlwyd. From the stream outflow, head west across grassy ground studded with smooth rocks. Numerous vague paths all converge and lead to a point beneath the broad spur of Y Gribin (the right-bounding ridge of the cwm).

Head along the well-used path that weaves its way up the left (east) flank of the spur. After climbing just over 200m the path arrives at large grassy plateau, known as 'the Football Field'. Cross to the south side of the grassy field and pick up a narrow path, which cuts up the hillside to the base of the rocky rib.

Description Starting from slightly right of the base, scramble up to the crest of the rib. Stay on the jagged crest for the duration of the ascent. There are intimidatingly big drops on the left (east) but there's always the option of a scrambly path not too far below on the right.

Descents or where next From the top of the rib, continue straight ahead to meet with the grassy ridge connecting the summit plateaus of Glyder Fach (head east) and Glyder Fawr (head west). The descent descriptions for Glyder Fach (994m) are given on page 95 and for Glyder Fawr (1001m) on page 128.

The broad spur of **Y Gribin** with its narrow upper rock rib visible on the skyline

Tania Scotland seeking out the best scrambling on the steeper left side of **Y Gribin's True Start.**

Y Gribin - True Start
Cwm Bochlwyd

25

Grade	1-
Area	Ogwen Valley
Aspect	Northeast (620m)
Approach	45 mins (653 590)

A nice enough scramble up the low-profile ridge that climbs southwest out of Cwm Bochlwyd. It provides a quiet, alternative approach to Y Gribin's (24) fine upper rock rib (this ridge is actually the rib's true continuation). The rock is sound but often lichenous, so the route is more enjoyable in dry conditions. The Main Cliff of Glyder Fach provides a dramatic backdrop and a detour onto this scramble may be worth it for this alone.

Approach Follow the approach described on page 89 to reach Llyn Bochlwyd. From the stream outflow, skirt leftwards around the lake. There is a faint but discernible track undulating between 10 and 20 metres above the shoreline, which will help keep your feet dry. Head for the indistinct beginnings of a low-profile ridge, approximately 125m from the southwest shore of the lake.

Description Head southwest up the broad lower part of the ridge. Initially it is just grass and heather with the occasional short section of rock, which can be creatively strung together.

Eventually the ridge steepens and the rock becomes more continuous. There is now a wide choice of scrambling lines. These are more interesting on the left, where the ridge overlooks the upper part of Cwm Bochlwyd. The ridge finally merges into Y Gribin, directly beneath its final narrow rock rib.

Descents or where next Continue along the crest of Y Gribin's upper rock rib (24). Or to descend, head northwest down a scree path to reach the grassy plateau of the Football Field. Cross to the northern end of the plateau, from where a good path, on the true right flank of the lower ridge, leads back to the outflow of Llyn Bochlwyd.

The view to the west from Glyder Fawr's summit plateau

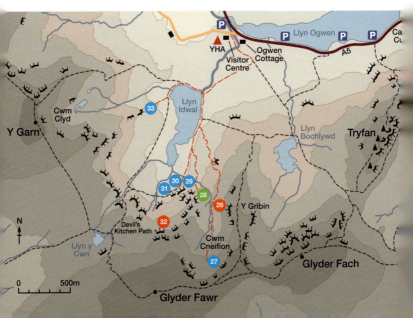

Cwm Idwal and Cwm Cneifion

Ogwen Valley

26	Cneifion Arête	3
27	Tower Rib	2
28	Seniors Gully	1-
29	Seniors Direct Approach	2
30	Idwal Staircase	2+
31	Idwal Buttress & Continuation	2
32	East Arête	3+
33	East Ridge of Y Garn	2

Cwm Idwal is a beautiful hanging valley, situated on the southern side of the Ogwen Valley, at the junction with the Nant Ffrancon, just above Ogwen Cottage. It is probably the most accessible high-mountain cwm in Wales and is extremely popular with just about anyone who likes walking in nice surroundings. There is a well-constructed circular path around the base of the cwm. This provides a fast, uncomplicated, feet-dry approach to all of the scrambles.

The left (east) side of the cwm is dominated by the long, sweeping northwest face of Glyder Fawr (1001m). At its base are the distinctive Idwal Slabs, which, with the exception of maybe one line, are just outside of the realms of scrambling territory. Above the slabs, the upper face comprises a series of walls and terraces. This, and just about everywhere right of here, is good scrambling terrain.

Two scrambles are described that climb the northwest face; Idwal Staircase (30) and Idwal Buttress (31). Although the descriptions for their starting sections are very prescriptive, the scrambles are open to variation once they reach the upper northwest face. The whole area is great for exploration, but it does require a keen nose for sniffing out a safe line.

Further to the right, and higher up, are the upper cliffs of Glyder Fawr, which are steeper and more broken than on the northwest face. This is a magical place, particularly in the evening sunshine, but good scrambling opportunities are limited. East Arête (32) is the only scramble described here. It is far superior to any other scrambling line on this impressive stretch of cliffs.

Ben Lawes in the enclosed cleft of the **Idwal Staircase**

Cwm Idwal and Cwm Cneifion

The rock on the east side of the cwm is invariably solid and reliable. It is typically slabby (alternating randomly between bum-cheek smooth and sandpaper rough), meaning that good balance and the ability to pad are often more useful than brute strength. This side of the cwm catches the afternoon and evening sun, and the rock dries super quick after any rain. If there's a breeze or sunshine, we're talking minutes rather than hours.

At the rear of the cwm, spread out above a long approach apron, is a shorter, darker band of cliffs. This is Clogwyn y Geifr. It is perpetually damp and heavily vegetated. It offers nothing that could be described as good scrambling. The cliffs are pierced at their centre by a prominent deep cleft, known as the Devil's Kitchen. To the left of the cleft, utilising a leftward rising ramp-line, is a path that climbs out of the cwm. The path connects with the expansive saddle separating Glyder Fawr and Y Garn and is often used for descent.

Y Garn (947m) is the shapely peak forming the right (west) side of Cwm Idwal. Its isolated summit gives one of the best views in the area. The mountain has two well-defined ridges that extend towards Cwm Idwal and cradle Cwm Clyd, a small bowl-shaped hanging valley. The left-hand (east) ridge supports a very prominent, sturdy-looking buttress, Castell y Geifr. The East Ridge (33) scramble offers a short but exciting ascent of this buttress and is sadly the only worthwhile route on this side of Cwm Idwal.

The Cwm Idwal aspect of Y Garn receives unrestricted sun from first thing in the morning, all year round. Low down, on its introductory rib, the rock can be quite greasy after extended periods of rain. However, any rock above the level of Llyn Clyd dries quickly and is rarely slippy.

Cwm Cneifion is the hanging valley above and to the southeast of Cwm Idwal. It is enclosed between Glyder Fawr's summit plateau and the west face of Y Gribin. It has an unusual 'out of the way' feeling. The periphery of the cwm is mostly a steep shattered and broken headwall. Two scrambles are described that safely climb through the headwall (others exist but are quite 'out there'). The Cneifion Arête (26) is every bit a classic and gets done in all weathers, throughout the year. Tower Rib (27) is pure esoterica. Due to its elevation and aspect, it is more of a fair weather outing.

Cwm Idwal and Cwm Cneifion

Ali Thomas lucky to catch the **Cneifion Arête** bathed in evening sun

Cneifion Arête

Cwm Cneifion

26

Grade	3
Area	Ogwen Valley
Aspect	West (750m)
Approach	45 mins (649 587)

A classic mountaineering line with the feel of an alpine ridge. Wonderfully airy, sensationally exposed and in a grand position high above Cwm Idwal. It is understandably a very popular objective, so if possible aim for an 'out of hours' visit. It captures the afternoon sun throughout the year and well into late evening in the summer. An ascent is feasible in any weather and thanks to an abundance of rock spikes and flakes, there's always a natural belay at hand, if a rope is required.

Approach From the visitor centre at Ogwen Cottage, follow the path that runs up and left from the entrance to the old slate cutting. After a few hundred metres the path curves back right and heads to the bridge at the outflow of Llyn Idwal. Take the path on the left side of the lake to a gate at a dry stone wall (the wall that runs into the lake).

After a further 20m, a stream crosses the path. From this point a grassy track runs diagonally rightwards up the hillside, ascends a steep patch of scree, then contours into Cwm Cneifion, the hanging valley perched up and left of Cwm Idwal. As the track enters the flat floor of Cwm Cneifion, the arête can be seen immediately on the left, a short way up the hillside. It is by far the most distinctive feature on the hillside, marking the right-hand edge of a large sweep of broken crag. A well-worn scree path zig-zags up to the base of the arête.

The arête can also be approached via any of the scrambles in Cwm Idwal. Although none offer the same grade of difficulty, Seniors Gully (28) is quick and nicely contrasting, whereas Idwal Staircase (30) provides the most continuous scrambling.

Cneifion Arête   Cwm Cneifion

Description Start just to the right of the toe of the arête. Ascend a rightward facing, shallow groove, until pushed right by some bulging rock. Head back left at the first opportunity, to gain a ledge nestled beneath a rightward leaning chimney. This first 20m of scrambling is steep and intimidating but there are plenty of good holds and it is not at all indicative of things to come.

Scramble up the rightward leaning chimney. This is slightly awkward but quickly leads to easier ground on the crest of the arête. The main difficulties are now behind and remainder of the route is pure joy. Continue upwards, over large spikes and flakes (often overhanging on the right) with the occasional nice slab thrown in for good measure. Ace!

Descents or where next The arête tops out on a large grassy plateau, known locally as 'the Football Field', high up on Y Gribin, the long ridge dropping from the eastern end of Glyder Fawr's plateau and separating Cwm Bochlwyd from Cwm Cneifion. For the easiest descent, head to the northern end of the plateau, from where a good path, on the true right flank of the lower ridge, leads to the outflow of Llyn Bochlwyd. A paved path then drops to the Ogwen Valley road.

Alternatively, cross to the southern end of the plateau and pick up a narrow path, which cuts up the hillside to the base of the upper rock rib on Y Gribin. Ascend the rib (24) to reach the broad grassy ridge that connects the summit plateaus of Glyder Fach (994m) and Glyder Fawr (1001m). The descent options from these summits are described on pages 95 and 128 respectively.

An excellent link-up is to combine the Cneifion Arête with an ascent of the Dolmen Ridge (23); two scrambles well-matched in difficulty and quality. From the top of the arête, head southeast across the Football Field, to reach its most easterly point. From here, pick a way down Y Gribin's True Start (25), which is easier on the true left. At the base of the steepening, contour southwest into upper Cwm Bochlwyd, aiming for a small pool (653 585).

From the pool, head across to the base of West Gully; the long depression running down the right-hand side of the main cliff, narrowing towards its base and with a broad scree fan beneath it. In poor visibility, a southeasterly bearing will take you directly to its entrance. The Dolmen Ridge begins at the toe of the quartz-marked rocks that form the left bounding wall of West Gully.

Ali Thomas scrambling along the wonderfully airy crest of **the Cneifion Arête**

Nigel Shepherd crossing the flat-topped pinnacle on the crest of **Tower Rib**

Leaving **Tower Rib** for the summit plateau of Glyder Fawr

Tower Rib

Cwm Cneifion

Grade	2
Area	Ogwen Valley
Aspect	Northwest (850m)
Approach	80 mins (648 582)

For seekers of solitude and a remote setting. It's a long way to walk for so little scrambling but this route just about warrants the effort. It tackles a solitary, steep rib protruding from an indistinct hillside, otherwise covered with shattered rock and semi-vegetated slabs. It is probably because this rib sits on its own, in such a high setting, that it is attractive. It gives an enlivening feeling of openness. And actually the scrambling isn't that bad either, just short.

Approach Follow the approach to Cwm Cneifion described on page 123, as for the Cneifion Arête (26). On reaching the flat floor of the cwm, head south and pick a way into the upper cwm. There are no tracks as such.

Tower Rib is located in the upper southeast area of the cwm, high on the shattered headwall and is relatively easy to find in good weather. It is distinguishable on approach as the route's culminating square-cut pinnacle breaks the otherwise uniform skyline of the cwm. From the floor of the cwm, it is the most conspicuous and continuous chunk of rock on the hillside. Another identifying feature is a gully (more than likely a stream) bounding its right side.

Conversely, in poor visibility it would be a nightmare to locate... and attempting the scramble in such conditions would be completely missing the point.

Tower Rib can also be approached via any of the scrambles in Cwm Idwal. Seniors Gully (28) being quick and nicely contrasting, whilst Idwal Buttress (31) has a very similar degree of difficulty.

Tower Rib   Cwm Cneifion

Description   The right bounding gully of Tower Rib runs down almost to the cwm floor but loses definition at the bottom. Ascend the vague, broken rib on the left of the gully.

The rib gradually steepens and narrows, as does the scrambling interest as height is gained. The first significant obstacle is turned on its left (start up a short corner then swing out left). Cut immediately back right across a slab to reach a position overlooking the gully. Head up the steep and sustained wall following the line of least resistance, first trending left then veering right, to reach the top of the rib.

Continue along the crest of the rib, climbing over the 4m high, flat-topped pinnacle (because it's there), to reach the plateau above the cwm headwall.

Descents or where next   The route tops out on the summit plateau of Glyder Fawr, approximately 700m east of the summit (1001m). The top of Glyder Fach (994m) is a similar distance away. Both summits offer extensive views and the entire plateau area of the Glyders is well worth taking the time to explore.

There are two equally scenic **descent options from Glyder Fawr**. The first is down Y Gribin (24), the long ridge dropping from the eastern end of Glyder Fawr's plateau and separating Cwm Bochlwyd from Cwm Cneifion. From the summit mound head in a easterly direction for a kilometre, to a large cairn marking the top of the ridge. To avoid all difficulties, take the rough, zig-zag scree path on the true left of the narrow, upper rock rib. Cross to the northern end of a large grassy plateau, known as 'the Football Field'. From where a good path, on the true right flank of the lower ridge, leads to the outflow of Llyn Bochlwyd. A paved path then drops to the Ogwen Valley road.

The second descent option is slightly longer but gives a more circular feel to the day's journey. Head southwest from the summit mound. After 75m, veer northwest and follow a series of large cairns to where the summit slopes begin to steepen and become heavily eroded. A deeply-scoured path then drops steeply rightwards, before zig-zagging down towards Llyn y Cwn.

At the bottom of the slope, when level with Llyn y Cwn, veer northeast and pick up the Devil's Kitchen path. The path enters a depression before curving steeply down to the true left, over a well-constructed section, beneath the cliffs of Clogwyn y Geifr. Continue down to meet with the circular path around Cwm Idwal.

Seniors Gully

Cwm Idwal

28

Grade	1-
Area	Cwm Idwal
Aspect	Northwest (530m)
Approach	35 mins (646 589)

An all-weather scramble. Probably better when it's raining… and definitely spooky if it's misty. The route ascends the gully connecting Cwm Idwal to Cwm Cneifion. It is overlooked on its right by the eastern retaining walls of the Idwal Slabs and their upper buttresses. This makes it a very sheltered scramble. There's also no exposure and there are good platforms and ledges between every rock step.

Approach From the visitor centre at Ogwen Cottage, follow the path that runs up and left from the entrance to the old slate cutting. After a few hundred metres the path curves back right and heads to the bridge at the outflow of Llyn Idwal. Take the path on the left side of the lake and continue for 500m, to where a large, conspicuous boulder sits 10m up from the path.

A few metres further along the path, from where a tiny stone bridge crosses a stream, a stony track runs diagonally rightwards up the hillside. Follow the track as it snakes its way across the hillside, to reach the beginnings of a wide couloir. This is more or less level with the upper limit of the East Wall (the steep retaining wall defining the left side of the Idwal Slabs). This particularly smooth upper section of the East Wall is also known as Suicide Wall.

Description Scramble up the wide couloir, picking a way through grass and heather, over short, easy rock steps. You'll eventually be channelled towards the looming cliffs on the right.

The wide couloir gradually becomes better defined and begins to feel more like a gully. The rocky steps become more continuous, but remain easy, with lots of rounded water-worn holds.

Zoe Wood and Catrin Smith behind the waterfall in **Seniors Gully**

Cwm Idwal Seniors Gully

Two thirds of the way up the gully is a small waterfall (behind which it's possible to stay dry). A rocky gangway to the left of the waterfall presents the only significant barrier on the scramble, where nippers may need some prudent spotting. Continue up the remains of the gully to emerge in the other world of Cwm Cneifion.

Descents or where next To return to Llyn Idwal, head northeast across the lip of the cwm, to a point just beyond the stream. Two paths originate in this area. A higher, easily visible track contours north, under the west flank of Y Gribin. Ignore this. Instead follow a lower, fainter path, which drops obliquely north before descending northwest, passing beneath the rocky spur of the Sub-Cneifion Rib.

Seniors Gully can be used as a more interesting approach to either of the Cwm Cneifion scrambles. For the Cneifion Arête (26), head east across the floor of the Cwm. The arête is by far the most distinctive feature on the hillside, marking the right-hand edge of a large sweep of broken crag. In poor visibility, look for a well-worn scree path, which zig-zags up to its base.

For Tower Rib (27), head southeast towards the high, shattered headwall of the cwm. The rib is distinguishable on the approach as the route's culminating square-cut pinnacle breaks the otherwise uniform skyline of the cwm. From the floor of the cwm, it is the most conspicuous and continuous chunk of rock on the hillside. Another identifying feature is a gully (more than likely a stream) bounding its right side. In poor visibility, well, good luck.

To continue to the summit of Glyder Fawr (1001m) from Seniors Gully, head up **Seniors Ridge**. The ridge extends north from Glyder Fawr's summit slopes and separates Cwm Idwal from Cwm Cneifion. Its crest is broad and gently angled throughout its entire length. A scruffy path picks a way through the ridge's numerous small rock bands, without encountering anything that would warrant a scrambling grade.

Start from behind the large, flat-faced boulder, which sits 10m above the exit to Seniors Gully. Follow the scruffy path as it meanders up the broad crest of the ridge, to where it merges into the mountain's stone-littered summit slopes. Continue across the open slopes, in a southwesterly direction, to the unusual summit mound. The two main descent options from Glyder Fawr's summit are described on page 128.

Paul James scrambling through the worn breach on East Wall, **Seniors Ridge Direct Approach**

Seniors Ridge Direct Approach

Cwm Idwal

29

Grade	2
Area	Ogwen Valley
Aspect	Northwest (460m)
Approach	25 mins (644 589)

A bitty scramble but okay nonetheless. Despite its commonly used name the route is anything but direct, taking a wandering line to connect the Cwm Idwal path with Seniors Ridge, the broad northeast spur of Glyder Fawr. The route's lower section ascends a series of cracks and grooves to the left of Idwal Slabs, these are often wet but not difficult. At halfway, an exposed and polished breach of the East Wall presents a definite crux. If this is too intimidating, the scramble can be abandoned here and swapped for an easier continuation up Seniors Gully (28).

Approach From the visitor centre at Ogwen Cottage, follow the path that runs up and left from the entrance to the old slate cutting. After a few hundred metres the path curves back right and heads to the bridge at the outflow of Llyn Idwal. Take the path on the left side of the lake, which passes directly underneath Idwal Slabs and continues in a circuit around Cwm Idwal.

Description Dropping off and defining the left side of Idwal Slabs is a steep retaining wall, known as the East Wall. The wall increases in height and becomes more imposing as it runs up the hillside. At the foot of the wall is a narrow, 20m high rectangular slab. Left of this is a lower, recessed slab split by a crack.

Head up the polished crack, veering left at its top to reach a grassy bay. From the rear of the bay follow a rightward veering groove, which passes between quartz slabs and steep vegetation, to arrive at an open grassy slope.

The route now follows a well-worn track up the grassy slope, which stays closely underneath the overshadowing East Wall. An awkward chimney adds a bit of spice.

The slabby start to Seniors Ridge Direct Approach

Continue up the track and over a few short steps, until the open slope becomes more of a couloir as steep slabby ground comes in from the left. Just above this point the East Wall can be breached, by following a rightward rising line of very polished holds (on an area of the wall almost denuded of vegetation). Head up the breach using the vertical 'letter box' feature on the left rather than the more tempting sloping ramps on the right. A wide, polished crack then leads to a large platform.

From the rear of the platform ascend a short wall, via rocky steps, to reach a flat, grassy area. A slabby spur then gives access to a higher grassy area, which in turn is exited via a steep, 4m high, pocketed wall. Follow a vague path into a tapering grassy alcove with a rough brown slab forming its left bounding wall. At the rear of the alcove scramble out left into Cwm Cneifion, to arrive at a flattening, between the exit of Seniors Gully (28) and the base of Seniors Ridge.

Descents or where next A description of the most logical descent route from this point, suggestions for linking to other scrambles, and an outline of how to continue to the summit of Glyder Fawr (1001m), are all given on page 131.

Idwal Staircase

Cwm Idwal

30

Grade	2+
Area	Ogwen Valley
Aspect	Northwest (450m)
Approach	25 mins (645 589)

A thoroughly satisfying scramble. The initial staircase section follows the cleaved fault line separating Idwal Slabs from Idwal Buttress. It is invariably wet, very wet, but this is all part of its elemental charm. The remainder of the scramble is a test of route finding ability, seeking out an easy passage through a maze of tiered rock barriers that form the upper northwest face of Glyder Fawr.

Approach From the visitor centre at Ogwen Cottage, follow the path that runs up and left from the entrance to the old slate cutting. After a few hundred metres the path curves back right and heads to the bridge at the outflow of Llyn Idwal. Take the path on the left side of the lake, which passes directly underneath Idwal Slabs and continues in a circuit around Cwm Idwal.

Description Start 30m past the right hand edge of Idwal Slabs, where a stream pours out from the bottom of the overhung gully (this could be bone dry during extended periods of no rain). Ascend to the right of the stream, using a series of flat, narrow ledges, to get established in the corner underneath the roof.

Head directly up the corner to a point where it curves left to meet the stream (jammed boulder under roof). Step or plough through the stream and continue scrambling upwards on its immediate left.

At the first sensible opportunity step right, back over the stream, or if the force of the water is too strong, trend further left towards easier, rougher rock. Whichever side of the stream you're on, continue up until the fault line opens out into a large, grassy flat area, level with the top of Idwal Buttress.

Ben Lawes ascending the water-washed corner of the **Idwal Staircase**

Follow a narrow, almost level track, traversing left across heather and grass, to the edge of a large area of tiered slabs. The trick now is to sniff out an easy passage through this maze of slabby rock. In general, a leftward-rising traverse, involving a sequence of corners, short slabs and quartz terraces, should eventually lead to a grassy mound. This is the highest point on this aspect of the face and the finish to the route.

Descents or where next To descend, head northeast down Seniors Ridge. Follow the scruffy path that meanders down the broad crest of the ridge, to a flattening in Cwm Cneifion. The flattening also marks the top of Seniors Gully (28). A description of the onward descent route from this point, plus suggestions for linking to other scrambles, are given on page 131. It is also possible to bail straight down Seniors Gully, which gives an uncomplicated scrambly descent, more or less directly to the base of the Idwal Slabs.

For the summit of Glyder Fawr (1001m), head southwest up Seniors Ridge, following the scruffy path on its broad crest, to where it merges into the mountain's stone-littered summit slopes. Continue across the open slopes, in a southwesterly direction, to the unusual summit mound.

Idwal Buttress & Continuation

Cwm Idwal

31

Grade	2
Area	Ogwen Valley
Aspect	Northwest (460m)
Approach	25 mins (644 589)

A fine, open scramble linking two buttresses of slabby rock, which at first do not seem likely partners. The initial section involves an ascent through the coarse, orange-tinted slabs of Idwal Buttress. A pleasant walk then connects with the contrasting smooth, grey slabs of the upper cliff of Glyder Fawr. Although disjointed and rambling in its mid section, the route feels like a very logical and complete line. The rock is excellent throughout.

Approach From the visitor centre at Ogwen Cottage, follow the path that runs up and left from the entrance to the old slate cutting. After a few hundred metres the path curves back right and heads to the bridge at the outflow of Llyn Idwal. Take the path on the left side of the lake and continue until underneath Idwal Slabs.

A further 30m to the right of the slabs is the unmistakable cleaved fault line of Idwal Staircase (30). This dark gully undercuts the pock-marked wall of Idwal Buttress, the long, rectangular buttress that appears to lean against the hillside. Continue along the path for a short distance until underneath the lowest rocks of the buttress.

Description Start directly under the buttress at a point where quartz bands meet the path. A grassy furrow splits the orange-tinted rock of the buttress. On the left of the furrow are short striated walls, on the right are blank slabs. Enter the furrow and follow broken rocky terrain to the top of the buttress.

Alternatively, trend left when level with the top of the striated walls to gain the left edge of the buttress. Pad delicately up the left side of the buttress, over beautiful, easy-angled slabs interspersed with useful slanting cracks. Recommended (grade 3).

Gav McGrath on the orange-tinted slabs of **Idwal Buttress**

Cwm Idwal — Idwal Buttress & Continuation

The flat top of the buttress continues as a blunt spur rising rightwards across the hillside. Follow the spur, scrambling over a couple of whaleback shaped, rocky mounds, until directly underneath the grassy couloir that descends from a distinctive notch on the skyline. A tongue of slabs bound the right of this couloir. Meander up to its tip (644 586).

Scramble straight up the tongue of slabs, cutting through a quartz band slightly left of centre (adjacent to a large boss of quartz). Above the quartz band is a platform, with a huge shard of rock lying at its right end. Leave the platform via a leftward rising rib, then veer further left over a final short slab to emerge just above the notch at the top of the grassy couloir.

Descents or where next To descend, head northeast down Seniors Ridge. Follow the scruffy path that meanders down the broad crest of the ridge, to a flattening in Cwm Cneifion. The flattening also marks the top of Seniors Gully (28). A description of the onward descent route from this point, plus suggestions for linking to other scrambles, are given on page 131. It is also possible to bail straight down Seniors Gully, which gives an uncomplicated scrambly descent, more or less directly to the base of the Idwal Slabs.

For the summit of Glyder Fawr (1001m), head southwest up Seniors Ridge, following the scruffy path on its broad crest, to where it merges into the mountain's stone-littered summit slopes. Continue across the open slopes, in a southwesterly direction, to the unusual summit mound. The two main descent options from Glyder Fawr's summit are described on page 128.

Konrad Doyle on the pinnacle of **East Arête** high above Cwm Idwal

East Arête

Cwm Idwal

Grade	3+
Area	Ogwen Valley
Aspect	North (750m)
Approach	50 mins (643 585)

A 'proper', adventurous mountain scramble, with a spectacular and commanding position high above Cwm Idwal. This is a serious route, particularly if you like the comfort of knowing a rope can be useful if things get tricky. Despite the rock being generally solid and reliable, there is a real scarcity of good belays. Perhaps this scramble should be reserved for the best of weathers, when you're going well and in a good frame of mind. Enigmatically described in an old guidebook as 'a worthy route to the summit if meditatively inclined'. You may well agree.

Approach The most logical approach is to follow the Idwal Buttress scramble (31) and only go as far as the top of the actual introductory buttress. The flat top of this buttress continues as a blunt spur rising rightwards across the hillside. Follow the spur, scrambling over a couple of whaleback shaped, rocky mounds, until it peters out into the hillside.

Continue rightwards underneath the lowest rocks of Glyder Fawr's upper cliff. Stop traversing when below the two horizontal quartz bands that mark the lowest point of a huge barrel-shaped buttress that is bounded on either side by a gully. This is East Buttress and its crest is East Arête (for reference, the wide grassy strip to its right, known as the High Pasture, is easily identifiable from the cwm floor).

East Arête can also be reached without a precursory scramble. From the visitor centre at Ogwen Cottage, follow the path that runs up and left from the entrance to the old slate cutting. After a few hundred metres the path curves back right and heads to the bridge at the outflow of Llyn Idwal. Take the path on the left side of the lake, continuing underneath Idwal Slabs, to reach a stream a few metres past the lowest rocks of Idwal Buttress. From here, head directly uphill following a steep scree chute to the base of East Buttress.

Konrad Doyle on the super smooth rib forming the base of **East Arête**

James Whitmore enjoying an autumnal inversion on Glyder Fawr's summit plateau

Cwm Idwal **East Arête**

Description Start at the lowest point on the buttress, immediately right of the two horizontal quartz bands. Ascend obliquely leftwards, passing underneath an obvious large area of clean, smooth slab. The left edge of the slab forms a well-defined rib of beautiful, compact rock. Move delicately up the rib using small, rounded but positive holds.

Eventually arrive at a very small ledge containing a narrow but distinct 2m long, horizontal quartz seam. This is the signal to start scrambling towards the centre of the buttress. So, shuffle delicately right for 4m to reach more secure ground.

Look up ahead and aim towards the pinnacle on the skyline. The scrambling is now a different flavour; easier and not so delicate but it does require some astute reading of the terrain to avoid possible dead ends.

Ascend the pinnacle direct (which of course isn't mandatory). The way ahead is now very easy, with the best of the remaining scrambling being to the left of the pinnacle over exposed blocky steps.

Descent or where next For the quickest descent, head east from the top of the arête. Continue along the cliff edge to where the top of Seniors Ridge merges into the summit slopes. A vague but discernible path originates at this point (645 584). Head northeast down the broad spur of Seniors Ridge, following a small weaving path, to arrive in Cwm Cneifion at a flattening, marking the intersection with the top of Seniors Gully (28).

Continue northeast, across the lip of Cwm Cneifion, to a point just beyond the stream. Two paths originate in this area. A higher, easily visible track contours north, under the west flank of Y Gribin. Ignore this. Instead follow a lower, fainter path, which drops obliquely north before descending northwest, passing beneath the rocky spur of the Sub-Cneifion Rib. Continue down the path to meet with circular path around Cwm Idwal

Alternatively (and why wouldn't you), to visit the top of Glyder Fawr (1001m), head south, over the stone-littered summit slopes. The mountain's unusual summit mound is less than 500m from the top of East Arête. The two main descent options from Glyder Fawr are described on page 128.

Ruth Bevan on an early morning ascent of the **East Ridge of Y Garn**

East Ridge of Y Garn

Cwm Idwal

33

Grade	2
Area	Ogwen Valley
Aspect	East (410m)
Approach	25 mins (642 597)

An impish buttress that livens up an otherwise easy ridge walk. This scramble heads up the left bounding ridge of Cwm Clyd, the hanging valley that dominates Y Garn's east face. A blast around the rim of this cwm is as natural a line as it gets and is one of the area's best short mountain trips, being easily achievable in less than half a day. Route finding is straightforward, it catches the sun throughout the morning and Y Garn's isolated summit gives out 360 degree views. Do it.

Approach From the visitor centre at Ogwen Cottage, follow the path that runs up and left from the entrance to the old slate cutting. After a few hundred metres the path curves back right and heads to the bridge at the outflow of Llyn Idwal.

Cross the bridge and follow the path around the right side of the lake to a narrow pebble beach. At the far end of the beach, pass through a gate in a stone wall and continue for a further 50m to where a stream crosses the path. This is the stream descending from Cwm Clyd.

Description Cross open ground to the base of the rib running down the left side of the stream. Scramble pleasantly up the rib, picking a way over easy rock steps interspersed by heathery walking. When the rib begins to flatten out and becomes more like the containing lip of the cwm, trend left towards the sturdy looking buttress of Castell y Geifr.

The front face of the buttress is steep and squat, with a shallow bay on its left-hand side. From within the bay, scramble steeply up to the left on good rock and, at the earliest opportunity, move back right to join the crest of a ridge.

East Ridge of Y Garn   Cwm Idwal

Scramble directly up the ridge (some loose rock but not worrying amounts), to reach an appreciably exposed level section. Walk carefully across this short, airy gangway to meet the first steepening, which can be ascended via a groove on its right.

The ridge narrows once again before reaching a second more imposing steepening. This is climbed on the right using vertical cracks and then an exposed step into a corner. The subsequent groove then leads back left, over large stacked blocks, to the top of the buttress and a fine viewpoint.

Continue around the rim of Cwm Clyd, up an easy walking slope, to the circular stone shelter on the summit of Y Garn (947m).

Descent or where next The natural descent is to continue round the rim of Cwm Clyd. To do this, firstly head down the blunt north ridge for 200m before turning right and following the good path down the slender crest of the northeast ridge. After dropping 100m, the ridge curves rightwards and continues descending to the floor of the cwm. A steep zig-zag path then leads back down to Cwm Idwal.

Alternatively, zoom down the broad southeast flank of Y Garn to Llyn y Cwn. Cross the outflow stream of the llyn and follow the Devil's Kitchen path, initially east then northeast, into a depression. The path then curves steeply down to the true left, over a well-constructed section, beneath the cliffs of Clogwyn y Geifr. Continue down to meet with the circular path around Cwm Idwal.

Cwm Idwal and the eastern aspect of Y Garn

Ruth Bevan cresting Castell y Ceifr on the **East Ridge of Y Garn**

Konrad Doyle on the knife-edged crest of **Pinnacle Ridge**

Pinnacle Ridge

Braich Ty Du, Pen yr Ole Wen

34

Grade	2
Area	Nant Ffrancon
Aspect	West (400m)
Approach	20 mins (649 611)

Quick and spectacular, a small taste of big exposure. This miniature scramble is nestled amongst the maze of rocky spurs and scree-filled gullies that litter the huge Braich Ty Du face of Pen yr Ole Wen. Despite its short length and low altitude, this ridge maxes out on excitement and provides surprisingly revealing views into the northern and eastern cwms of the Glyders. Views so expansive, they would normally belong to much higher vantage points.

Approach From the visitors centre at Ogwen Cottage, or any of the other nearby parking areas in the Ogwen Valley, walk along the road to the bridge spanning the waterfalls on the river emerging from Llyn Ogwen. Cross the Alf Embleton stile on the north side of the river, turn immediately left and follow the rough path up to a grassy shoulder.

Sitting just off the top of the shoulder are three unusual, circular stone-built pens, without entrances. Looking down the Nant Ffrancon valley the petite Pinnacle Ridge, topped by its two distinctive pinnacles, is now clearly visible on the hillside to your right.

From the circular pens, follow a good track northeast that contours the hillside staying approximately 30m above the road. Stop after 350m, where the track passes beneath a rocky spur that extends low down the hillside - at its bottom is an almost flat-faced buttress with a band of small roofs at half height. If you arrive at a rock-fall barrier fence you've gone 50m too far.

Head straight up the heathery hillside, turning the flat-faced buttress on its right. A steep scree path soon materialises, which runs up the right-hand side of the spur into a heather and debris filled couloir. A few minutes of steep walking brings you to an old stone wall that spans the couloir and lies directly underneath Pinnacle Ridge (above on your left).

Description Start approximately 10m below the stone wall, from where a distinctive depression leads up to the crest of the ridge. Easy scrambling over ledges leads up to a short wall. Ascend the wall, then follow the crest to reach a ledge at the base of the first pinnacle.

Pass the first pinnacle on its right and the second pinnacle bravely on its left (spectacularly exposed and extremely photogenic). Scramble over a final 2m step onto a long, flat shoulder and a fine viewpoint.

Descents or where next Continue along the shoulder and descend a narrow track on the right into the upper part of the heather and debris filled couloir. Head down the couloir to regain the scree path used on the ascent before tootling back across the hillside towards Ogwen Cottage.

It is perfectly feasible to continue up through the Braich Ty Du face towards the summit of Pen yr Ole Wen. There is some reasonably good scrambling amongst the cluster of rocky ribs on the upper left of the face, although reaching them does involve a fair amount of heather bashing and is best done when visibility isn't hampered. A keen sense of exploration will come in handy.

South Arête

Foel-goch

35

Grade	1+
Area	Nant Ffrancon
Aspect	Northeast (510m)
Approach	30 mins (635 611)

Esoteric rambling amid the maze of small outcrops and miniature towers forming the left edge of Creigiau Gleision; an obscure and curious crag tucked up on the hillside on the west of the Nant Ffrancon. The route offers little in the way of quality scrambling, but it does have its moments - in fact a pioneering approach is called for. Do expect an abundance of atmosphere, which is what this scramble is all about. Some of the rock requires care.

Approach From Ogwen Cottage head down the old Nant Ffrancon road, continuing 350m past the scout hut at Yr Hafod to a stone bridge (642606), just before the road drops steeply to Blaen-y-nant. From the bridge, follow a faint path (very faint at times) running diagonally rightwards up the hillside. At a point just above a small crag, the path intersects with a much more established traversing path. Follow this better path rightwards as it initially contours around the hillside, then gains height to arrive just beneath the cliffs.

It's worth noting there is a good path connecting Cwm Idwal to Cwm Cywion, which then continues on to a collection of sheepfolds on the flattening below eastern end of Creigiau Gleision. The approach starts at the outflow of Llyn Idwal and initially follows the path leading up to Y Garn's northeast ridge (marked on the 1:25000 OS map). It then sidles under Pinnacle Crag, sticking to the uphill side of the highest stone wall as it contours underneath the scattered outcrops of the Mushroom Garden. Although much longer, this is a very easy and scenic approach to Creigiau Gleision.

The cliffs at the eastern end of Creigiau Gleision appear as a chaotic sprawl of small buttresses, interspersed by serrated arêtes and scree chutes. The broken ridge forming the left edge of the crag is South Arête. The conspicuous, deep gully immediately to the right of South Arête is East Gully.

Ric Potter skipping along the final narrow stretch of **Foel-goch's South Arête**

The profile of **South Arête** on the approach from Blaen-y-nant

Foel-goch South Arête

Description Head up the grassy slope on the left of the scree runnel beneath East Gully, until a buttress forces you into the gully bed. Pick a way up the loose ground of the gully bed for 40m, until stopped by a rock barrier and a path cutting across the gully. The path links grassy saddles on the left and right skylines.

Gain the grassy saddle on the left, which puts you on the broad, open crest of South Arête. Quest uphill, choosing the most interesting line through the succession of small outcrops and towers, all the while keeping East Gully close to your right.

After a while, the outcrops converge to become more recognisable as a ridge. Scramble a short distance, along the crest if possible, until stopped by a steep tower. Bypass the tower on the left, stepping over an incongruous miniature stone wall, and regain the crest of the ridge via a notch containing a chockstone.

A final difficult buttress can be avoided on its right by traversing into East Gully at a point just above a steepening in the gully bed. Head up the gully to the top of the crag. Alternatively, ascended the buttress on its left (marginally increasing the route's overall grade) and continue to the top of the crag via a short, exposed ridge.

Descent or where next The quickest and a very easy descent is to follow a narrow path that drops southeast into Cwm Cywion (the path passes within a few metres of the top of the scramble). From the wall crossing the lower cwm, a number of faint tracks head down the hillside back to the old Nant Ffrancon road. The best of these originate at the small ravine.

If time allows, a visit to the summit of Foel-goch (831m), followed by a high level return route to Ogwen Cottage, is highly recommended. From the top of the scramble head west up the ridgeline, then veer northwest along the cliff tops to the summit. To return, walk south for a kilometre before ascending southeast to the circular stone shelter and a fine viewpoint on the summit of Y Garn (947m). Descend the broad southeast flank of Y Garn to Llyn y Cwn.

Cross the outflow stream of the llyn and follow the Devil's Kitchen path, initially east then northeast, into a depression. The path then curves steeply down to the true left, over a well-constructed section, beneath the cliffs of Clogwyn y Geifr. Continue down to meet with the circular path around Cwm Idwal.

Sheila van Lieshout getting the scrambling thing on **Foel-goch's North Arête**

North Arête

Foel-goch

36

Grade	2+
Area	Nant Ffrancon
Aspect	Northeast (510m)
Approach	30 mins (635 611)

A gem of a scramble. Superb positions, continuously interesting and with good rock too. Set amongst a fascinating sprawl of irregular shaped pinnacles and buttresses, it is steeped in atmosphere. Who cares if it isn't that long? There is an uncanny charm to this route that has little to do with the quality of its scrambling. Best done in dry conditions. But being an exposed ridge, it does dry quickly after rain.

Approach Follow either of the approaches to Creigiau Gleison, as described on page 151. The cliffs at the eastern end of the crag appear as a chaotic sprawl of small buttresses, interspersed by serrated arêtes and scree chutes. The conspicuous, deep gully towards the left of this sprawl is East Gully. The ridge bounding the right-hand side of the gully is North Arête. It is the central and best defined of the three ridges in this east facing area of the crag.

Description Start in a wide grassy recess approximately 50m to the right of East Gully. The recess is deep enough that it could easily be classed as a gully (let's say it's on the cusp). There is a house-sized quartz-topped buttress standing on the right of its entrance.

Head into the recess and look up and right for a small, compact crag of clean rock that is undercut on the right and displays a rightward leaning quartz stripe. Sneak behind this crag on the right and cut back left into a broad grass and heather filled couloir. Pick a way easily up the couloir, or climb the scrappy rib on the left, to reach a shelf on North Arête that overlooks East Gully.

The way ahead, up the arête, is blocked by a steep, intimidating wall. Creep around to the right, beneath a bulge, to where a heather-filled runnel (serious if wet) leads up to a distinctive notch, back on the crest of the arête.

Sheila van Lieshout crossing the pinnacles on **North Arête**

The eastern cliffs of Creigiau Gleision seen from the Nant Ffrancon

Foel-goch North Arête

Scramble steeply out of the notch via an exposed slab on the left, then continue along the narrow crest to reach a tower with a hole through its base; a feature that gives the route its other name of 'Needle's Eye Arête'

Climb the tower direct by a steep chimney or shuffle around to the left and regain the crest via a short but equally steep wall. Continue more easily along the crest of the arête tackling a succession of funky pinnacles, all of which can be bypassed if wished.

The arête soon peters out into a broad bilberry-covered shoulder. This feels like the end of the arête and the route can be finished here by following a faint grassy track that leads out rightwards to the top of the crag.

It is only in retrospect, when looking down, that the natural line of the arête can be seen to actually continue, up and left from the bilberry-covered shoulder. The scrambling on this short continuation is fun but a grade harder.

From the shoulder, walk across to the base of a small left-facing slab and nip delicately up its right edge. Ahead stands a final fin of rock. Don't be tempted to venture onto the obvious pedestal on the fin's nose. Instead, shuffle out onto the front of the fin along a higher, leftward-rising ledge that gives access to some positive hand holds. A few very exposed moves lead to the top of the fin and the end of the scrambling.

Descent or where next Follow either of the descent options for Foel-goch's South Arête (35), as described on page 153.

An interesting link-up is to follow North Arête with an ascent of Atlantic Ridge (37). Despite being very contrasting scrambles, they strangely complement each other and create an excellent excursion around the Nant Ffrancon. From the top of North Arête, head west up the ridgeline, then veer northwest along the cliff tops to the summit Foel-goch. Descend northwest to intersect with a well-established path, which is followed north towards Mynydd Perfedd.

From the summit of Mynydd Perfedd, descend northeast and trace the cliff edge to the grassy promontory overlooking the south bounding ridge of Cwm Graianog. Pick a way down the ridge, which tends to be easier on the true right. Where the ridge steepens, veer sharply to the true right. On reaching easy ground beneath the lowest outcrops on the ridge, contour around the floor of the cwm towards the base of the Atlantic Slabs.

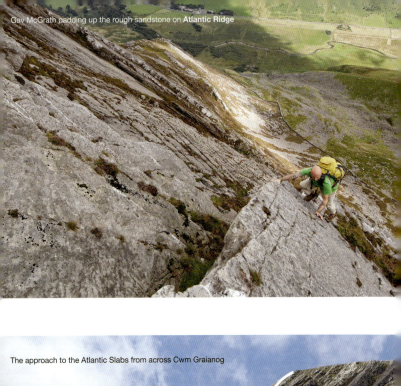
Gav McGrath padding up the rough sandstone on **Atlantic Ridge**

The approach to the Atlantic Slabs from across Cwm Graianog

Atlantic Ridge

Carnedd y Filiast

37

Grade	3
Area	Nant Ffrancon
Aspect	Southwest (650m)
Approach	60 mins (623 627)

A unique outing with an extraordinary sense of space. This scramble creeps up the edge of a 250m slab, one of a group of long sandstone faces known collectively as the Atlantic Slabs. These expansive sweeps of rock are situated high on Carnedd Y Filiast, a seemingly neglected peak lying above the northern end of the Nant Ffrancon. The route ascends solid, roughly textured rock, and is not particularly difficult for its grade. However, it is quite committing and despite its easy angle, would be tricky to abandon.

Approach From Ogwen Cottage, head 3km down the old Nant Ffrancon road to the Tai-newyddion outdoor centre. There are parking spaces in a small lay-by 150m before (south of) Tai-newyddion or on the verge just past the centre itself.

A no-nonsense approach into Cwm Graianog and the Atlantic Slabs is to cross the stile to the right of Tai-newyddion, skirt around the building and follow the overly engineered stone wall on its uphill side into the cwm.

From a point where the wall is straddled by some huge boulders, head uphill following a wide scree and boulder fan. This boulder fan emanates from a deep, crescent shaped gully forming the left bounding edge of the true Atlantic Slab; the largest of all the slabs. The Atlantic Ridge scramble takes the right bounding edge of this huge slab, to the right of which is a series of overlaps.

A far more aesthetic approach, and allowing you to better scope out the layout of the slabs, is to head directly up the hillside from a cattle grid 250m south of Tai-newyddion. The ascent is very steep but dry underfoot. Once the open cwm floor is reached, pass a romantically shaped sheep pen and head for the boulders that straddle the stone wall, as previously described.

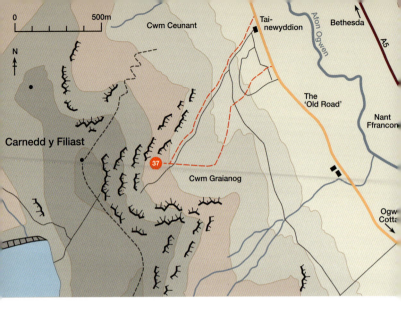

Description Start from the lowest part of the slab, at its bottom right-hand corner. Initially easy and interspersed by bands of heather, the ridge soon starts to become more interesting. Keep to the right edge as much as possible, linking small slabs and ribbons of rock, and occasionally bobbing around the overlap to keep the scrambling continuous.

At half height the angle eases slightly and the quality of the scrambling improves, particularly on the clean right edge. The expansive nature of the slabs can now be really appreciated. Continue, without any surprises, to the top of the slab. There are stacks of belays throughout should the comfort of a rope ever be needed.

Descents or where next The rocky summit of Carnedd y Filiast (821m) is just over 100m west from the highest point of the slabs. The quickest descent is to head northeast from the summit, avoiding the rough ground of a tempting direct line to Tai-newyddion.

Carnedd y Filiast **Atlantic Ridge**

The most scenically rewarding descent is by the south bounding ridge of Cwm Graianog. Head southeast from the summit of Carnedd y Filiast and trace the cliff edge to the grassy promontory overlooking the ridge. Pick a way down the ridge, which tends to be easier on the true right. Towards the bottom of the ridge, where it steepens, veer sharply to the true right.

Starting the day by walking from Ogwen Cottage has the benefit of an excellent high-level return route, across the four principal tops of the northern Glyders. This is also the logical return route if Atlantic Ridge was preceded by an ascent of North Arête (36).

Head southeast from the summit of Carnedd y Filiast and follow the broad ridgeline to Mynydd Perfedd (812m). From here, descend southeast to cross the narrow saddle that leads to the grassy slopes of Foel-goch. Continue over Foel-goch (831m) or follow the well-established path that skirts around its right (west) flank. Both options converge at the col beneath the northwest ridge of Y Garn (947m). A stiff walk leads up to the circular summit shelter.

Descend the broad southeast flank of Y Garn to Llyn y Cwn. Cross the outflow stream of the llyn and follow the Devil's Kitchen path, initially east then northeast, into a depression. The path then curves steeply down to the true left, over a well-constructed section, beneath the cliffs of Clogwyn y Geifr. Continue down to meet with the circular path around Cwm Idwal.

Bone dry conditions for Mark Lynden in the long central section of **Bryants Gully**

Bryants Gully

Glyder Fawr / Llanberis Pass

38

Grade	3-
Area	Llanberis Pass
Aspect	Southwest (280m)
Approach	15 mins (626 571)

An enchanting journey through the snaking watercourse that splits the southwest flank of Glyder Fawr. The route is over 500m long, starting as a well-defined gully just above the valley floor and finishing as a rocky couloir on the skyline cliffs, high above the north side of Llanberis Pass. Difficulties are short but are poorly protected; if at all. The upper half of the route is prone to stone fall, so caution is needed if there is a team above. Better than any ghyll scramble in the Lake District.

Approach There are a number of parking spots in the Llanberis Pass. The most convenient are the small Ynys Ettws lay-by (626 568) or the larger lay-by further west (621 571), directly below Clogwyn y Grochan. From the Ynys Ettws lay-by, cross the road and follow a narrow leftward rising trail to reach the right-hand end of Carreg Wastad (the rectangular crag 120m up the hillside with a lush grassy couloir tucked to its right). From the Grochan lay-by, walk 200m east (a vague track on the north side of the road), then pick a rising diagonal line, up grassy slopes, to the terrace beneath Carreg Wastad. From the right-hand end of the crag, trend up and right for 80m to where a stream issues from the base of a tree-filled gully.

Description Scramble up the stream bed to the large rectangular boulder that blocks the narrow gully. Bypass the boulder via a smooth slab on the left. If the slab proves to be too greasy, retrace the gully to a point 5m below the boulder and climb out easily to the left. Continue up to reach a peaceful, tree-covered ravine. Above the ravine, the route continues as a narrow gully and involves nice scrambling over sizeable, jammed boulders and blocks. The largest boulder (undercut with a small cave at its base) is passed steeply on the left, using large, friendly holds not immediately visible from below.

Bryants Gully Glyder Fawr / Llanberis Pass

The gully's initial narrow section ends abruptly and the route opens up into a grassy amphitheatre with a small waterfall at its rear. Scramble up to the right of the waterfall and follow the now wider watercourse through the heather-covered hillside.

Bridge up a constriction containing a jammed boulder and enter a steep-sided alcove. At first the alcove seems like a dead end. However, an escape is possible by climbing the right wall, starting approximately 3m from the rear of the alcove, then scrambling up in a one o'clock direction. The wall is steep but has small, positive holds. The escape can be quite exciting if wet.

Enter a second alcove, which is easily escaped by following the line of the watercourse. Continue up a v-shaped gully into a third alcove with unusual undercut columns of rock forming its left bounding wall. Escape from the alcove by climbing the concrete-textured wall on the right, starting approximately 10m from the rear of the alcove.

Having escaped the final alcove, follow a rightward curving groove through some quite special rock architecture (best appreciated by looking back down the gully). A thin rock rib soon divides the way ahead. Scramble through the narrow gully on the right of the rib, to reach a broad couloir filled with orange scree. Ignore the scree-filled couloir, instead carefully ascend the shattered rib on its left.

The rib soon peters out into easier-angled slopes beneath the cliffs of Esgair Felen; the broad southwest spur of Glyder Fawr. Standing in the centre of the cliffs is a tall, conspicuous arête. Beneath the arête, on either side, are two large bays. Walk up over shattered ground, heading for the right-hand bay. Scramble up through the bay and enter a narrow, chossy couloir (hidden to the right of the arête). The couloir emerges onto the grassy, flat top of Esgair Felen.

Descents or where next For the summit of Glyder Fawr (1001m), walk northeast for 1.3km, to meet with a well-used, cairned path. Follow the path southeast, up to the summit mound. To descend, retrace the cairned path and head northwest to where the summit slopes begin to steepen and become heavily eroded. A deeply-scoured path then drops steeply rightwards, before zig-zagging down towards Llyn y Cwn. From the llyn, follow the Cwm Padrig footpath southwest, back down to the Llanberis Pass. A quicker but much rougher descent into Cwm Padrig, via a steep scree slope, is possible from the vicinity of the 800m contour on Esgair Felen.

Matt Hawkins deep inside the central couloir of Esgair Felen. **Bryants Gully**

Paul Dickson in the slippery depths of **Jammed Boulder Gully**

Jammed Boulder Gully

Dinas Mot / Llanberis Pass

39

Grade	3+
Area	Llanberis Pass
Aspect	North (330m)
Approach	20 mins (625 563)

A scramble to be reckoned with. The main challenge isn't the high degree of technical difficulty; it is more often coping with the gully's inherent slipperiness. In anything but the driest conditions, think really hard before attempting this route alone... besides, for a scramble like this, team tactics are really where the fun lies. It's worth noting that to abseil from this scramble and not have to leave your rope behind, a 50m length is required.

Approach From the Cromlech Boulders lay-by (628 567), cross the river and head south across open ground, aiming for the last stile on the wall to the left, running uphill. Cross the stile and follow the zig-zag path, which runs steeply up through scree to the base of 'the nose' of Dinas Mot. Contour to the right, following a vague track for 200m, until underneath the first significant recess in the cliff. Set back, in the rear of the recess, is an isolated buttress. The buttress is defined on each side by a deep gully. Head to the entrance of the left-hand gully, which is further identified, strangely enough, by a huge jammed boulder at mid-height.

Description Scramble up over slimy ground to where the gully steepens abruptly. Step out right via some very tenuous moves, and then inch up to a stance directly below the jammed boulder. This innocuous section can be the crux of the whole route and absolutely desperate if the slime is out in force.

Enter the cave and work your way up and left towards the daylight in the roof (making sure you're facing the correct way and having organised any rucksack logistics in advance). Pop out onto a spacious, grassy platform.

On the wall to the right, 4m from the rear of the platform, is a smooth ramp line. Scramble carefully up the ramp to reach an upper bay.

Dinas Mot and the approach to **Jammed Boulder Gully**

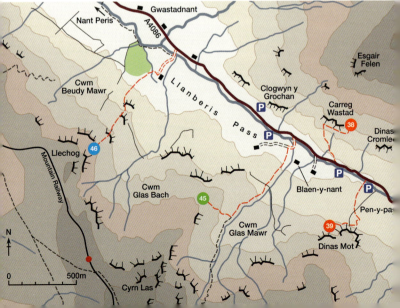

Dinas Mot / Llanberis Pass — **Jammed Boulder Gully**

Escape the upper bay at its rear by shimmying through a gap behind a small jammed block, an effort that is fully in keeping with the gully's previous squeeze. Alternatively, if dry, a much easier escape is by the wall on the right; starting 4m from the rear of the bay and taking a rising leftward line. Easy scrambling up the remaining short runnel leads to wide grassy terraces.

Descent or where next To descend, head left (east) along terraces and ledges, occasionally gaining height to avoid the edge of the crag. After approximately 250m, head down a rough track in a broad scree-filled depression, which leads to the base of the crag.

Jammed Boulder Gully makes an excellent prelude to either the North Ridge of Crib Goch (41) or the Clogwyn y Person Arête (44). From the grassy terraces at the top of the gully, head upwards, picking a way through the small rock barriers covering the convex hillside. The hillside soon levels out and tapers to form a broad grassy shoulder. Continue along the shoulder to reach the base of the North Ridge of Crib Goch.

Approximately 50m above the shoulder, on the broad base of the North Ridge, is a small grassy terrace. The terrace supports the Fox's Path, which at this point is quite faint. Contour around to the right (west swinging to south), along the faint path, which rises gently across patches of scree into Cwm Uchaf. Cross the undulating floor of the cwm to the snout of smooth rock forming the base of the Clogwyn y Person Arête.

Although only a short distance, crossing the floor of Cwm Uchaf can be very disorientating in poor visibility. It may be easier to head west along the lip of the cwm, over easy ground, to reach Llyn Glas. A southwesterly bearing will then lead directly up to the base of the arête.

Early morning light spreading across the east flank of Crib Goch

Crib Goch and Crib y Ddysgl

Snowdon Group

40	**East Ridge**	1
41	**North Ridge**	1
42	**Main Ridge Traverse**	1
43	**Crib y Ddysgl**	1
44	**Clogwyn y Person Arête**	3
45	**Cwm Glas Spur**	1-
46	**Llechog Buttress**	2

Crib Coch (923m) and Crib y Ddysgl (1065m) lie just north of Snowdon (Yr Wyddfa in Welsh,1085m) and are characterised by their long summit ridges and impressive north facing cwms. Along with Lliwedd (898m), these four mountains encircle the lakes of Llyn Llydaw and Glaslyn, and are often collectively referred to as the Snowdon Horseshoe.

Seen from Pen-y-pass, **Crib Goch** appears as a great pyramid. Every bit a proper mountain, in both form and scale. The summit in view is the East Summit. It is a few metres lower than the true summit but naturally feels like the top of the mountain, and this is how it is generally perceived. It is the converging point of the mountain's three ridges. The left-hand skyline is the East Ridge and sweeping down on the right is the North Ridge. The famous knife-edged Main Ridge is out of sight on the far side of the mountain.

Crib Goch's flanks are invariably rotten, comprised of loose rock and scree, and are not pleasant places to wander onto. Only the ridges provide safe routes to the mountain's summits and each of these ridges involves very exposed scrambling. In fact, Crib Goch is unique in being the only Welsh mountain that doesn't have an easy walking route to its top.

The East Ridge accounts for the vast majority of ascents of Crib Goch. After ascending the East Ridge most people will then continue westwards, along the Main Ridge. This is undoubtedly because these two ridges form the first stage in the classic circuit of the Snowdon Horseshoe, and have become considered as the 'normal way' to traverse the mountain. Comparatively, the North Ridge, used either in ascent or descent, gets very little attention. As a consequence, the wilder side of the mountain remains undiscovered by many.

Crib Goch and Crib y Ddysgl

The scorched landscape of the Snowdon group during a severe spring drought.

40	East Ridge	1
41	North Ridge	1
42	Main Ridge	1
43	Crib y Ddysgl	1
44	Clogwyn y Person Arête	3

Crib Goch and Crib y Ddysgl

Crib Goch is very susceptible to poor weather and a strong wind from any direction will indiscriminately whip around the mountain. Normal mountaineering logic, which steers us towards sheltered aspects, goes out the window. It doesn't apply that in a westerly wind, the East Ridge will be sheltered. Or in a southerly, that the North Ridge will be sheltered. Crib Goch's topography gives very little protection from the elements from whichever direction they are coming. Winds also have a tendency to accelerate up the mountain's uniform slopes and howl across very localised points on the Main Ridge, at speeds far in excess of the day's forecast. So in a nutshell, think carefully before heading up Crib Goch on even a moderately windy day.

It is a myth that Crib Goch is always a 'busy' mountain. Yes, between 9am and midday on any weekend, or Bank Holiday, a long line of people will be slowly inching their way across the Main Ridge. However, once those on a mission to complete the Snowdon Horseshoe have passed, afternoons will seem relatively quiet. And on any evening, scrambling on Crib Goch is always a tranquil affair; with every likelihood you will be crossing the mountain without any other parties in sight.

Crib y Ddysgl could easily be eclipsed by the grandeur of Snowdon, when in fact it is an infinitely more interesting mountain to explore. It is marked as 'Garnedd Ugain' on the current 1:25000 OS map but it is more commonly referred to by its original name.

The mountain is primarily known for the narrow, kilometre long ridge, extending east towards Crib y Goch. The ridge forms the second stage in the circuit of the Snowdon Horseshoe. As good as it is, for most visitors the ridge will sadly be their only experience of such a grand mountain.

Crib y Ddysgl's south flank is similar to that of Crib Goch's; uniformly steep, loose and uninviting. Conversely, its north facing cwms are fascinating in their complexity and in their abundance of buttresses and crags. The feeling of wildness and solitude experienced within these cwms is quite exceptional, especially considering their relative proximity to the hubbub that often surrounds Snowdon. Three scrambles are described that start within these cwms, from which the Cwm Glas Spur (45) stands out as a must-do route. It is within everyone's capability and is simply an incredibly scenic way to the mountain's summit.

East Ridge

Crib Goch

40

Grade	1
Area	Snowdon Group
Aspect	East (750m)
Approach	45 mins (628 552)

A first-rate scramble, direct to a fantastic summit. There is always something special about scrambling to the top of a classically shaped peak and this outing is no exception. The broad lower half of the ridge can be ascended by a number of lines. All the variations converge in the upper half, where the angle eases and the scrambling turns into an airy ridge walk. The rock is generally okay, so long as the flanks are avoided. This is the first scramble in the classic circuit of the Snowdon Horseshoe.

Approach Park at Pen-y-pass (car park usually full by 8am at weekends) or in the free lay-bys (665 559) on the A4086, east of the Pen y Gwryd Hotel, just over the Conwy County border. There is also a park-and-ride scheme operating from Nant Peris but the timetable is very limited outside peak holiday periods.

From Pen-y-pass head west along the Pyg Track to the prominent col of Bwlch y Moch. The bwlch is where the path to Crib Goch splits off. It is also the first viewpoint for Snowdon, Lliwedd and Llyn Llydaw. Take the right-hand path, which meanders up the hillside, over short scrambly steps, towards the East Ridge. The path stops on a broad shoulder beneath a steep band of rock, which runs around the base of the blunt ridge.

Description There are a number of possible scrambling lines through the initial band of steep rock. The more well-used and solid options are within a 30m vicinity of the blunt nose of the ridge. Don't be tempted to stray outside this area as the rock quality deteriorates rapidly. Very Rapidly.

Dave Noddings on the finishing crest of the **East Ridge of Crib Goch**

The shallow depression in the lower half of the **East Ridge of Crib Goch**

Crib Goch **East Ridge**

From a ledge above the initial barrier, scramble up a shallow depression for 60 metres or so, to reach the easier-angled and narrower upper section of the ridge. If wet, the smooth polished rock in the depression can feel a tad slippy. More positive but steeper lines can be found on the rock to the left.

On the upper part of the ridge shattered rock steps lead up to a fine exposed crest. Avoid the small paths that sidle across the right (north) flank. Keep to the crest where the rock is more reliable. Continue to the East Summit.

Descent or where next The majority of people will likely continue along the Main Ridge (42), as this is the next step in the circuit of the Snowdon Horseshoe. It's also possible to traverse the Main Ridge then return to Pen-y-pass, without any necessity to continue around the horseshoe. This is done by dropping left (south) from Bwlch Goch, the col between Crib Goch and Crib y Ddysgl, to meet with the Pyg Track, and is described on page 186.

A descent of the North Ridge (41) makes an excellent, shorter, and what could be considered 'alternative', traverse of the mountain. From the East Summit head north, sticking to the crest of the knife-edged ridge. The knife-edge is short lived. However, there is a short, exposed down-climb into a niche before the broader, easier section of the ridge can be reached.

Walk down the shattered crest of the ridge. At its natural end, where the ridge broadens and becomes less defined, continue in the same direction, dropping down a steep, dirt slope. After descending approximately 50m there is a small, grassy ledge (at the 700m contour line). The ledge supports the Fox's Path (page 186). Head southeast along the path, which contours across the northeast face of Crib Goch, back towards the base of the East Ridge.

Alternatively, for a very scenic descent to the Llanberis Pass, stop approximately 50m before the natural end of the North Ridge. From here, a well-used scree path on the true left flank drops into Cwm Uchaf. The layout of the cwm is complex and the onward descent involves negotiating some very steep ground, which can be tricky in poor visibility.

The safest descent is by a rough, stony path starting on the western side of the cwm, beyond Llyn Glas. The path drops into Cwm Glas Mawr by following a line that stays approximately 30m from the true right of the stream coming from Llyn Bach. Once in Cwm Glas Mawr, a much better path on the true left bank of the stream leads down to the Pass.

Sarah and Ian Ridgway on a spring evening run along **Crib Goch's North Ridge**

The elegant line of **Grib Goch's North Ridge** seen from the Dinorwig Quarries

North Ridge

Crib Goch

41

Grade	1
Area	Snowdon Group
Aspect	North (700m)
Approach	60 mins (625 557)

A beautiful mountain ridge and the most aesthetically pleasing line in North Wales. The route is predominantly a ridge walk that culminates in a short but very exposed scramble along a knife-edged crest. The rock is mainly shattered and loose but becomes more reliable during the short scrambling section. As with the East Ridge, this scramble leads directly to Crib Goch's fantastic East Summit. Access to the base of the ridge is much easier than a map would suggest.

Approach An easy, very scenic, but rather circuitous approach starts in the Llanberis Pass. The most convenient parking is at the large lay-bys (621 571) situated on both sides of the road, below Clogwyn y Grochan. Cross the river using the nearby small vehicular bridge at Blaen-y-nant (623 570) and continue straight ahead. After 50m, turn right over a second bridge and head up a good path on the right (west) side of the stream.

Follow the right (west) bank of the river across Cwm Glas Mawr towards the impressive crags beneath Cyrn Las. A steep stony path picks a way up the hillside to the left of crags. Head up the path and at the top of the rise veer left, towards Llyn Glas, a small lake with an island, nestled in the entrance to Cwm Uchaf. From the lake, head east, across grassy slopes and rock slabs forming the lip of the cwm. After 500m reach the west flank of the North Ridge, near its base.

A quicker approach, and perhaps more logical if a descent of the East Ridge is planned, starts at Pen-y-pass. From the car park, head west along the Pyg Track to the prominent col of Bwlch y Moch. The bwlch is where the path to Crib Goch splits off. It is also the first viewpoint for Snowdon, Lliwedd and Lyn Llydaw. Take the right-hand path, which meanders up the hillside, over short scrambly steps, towards the East Ridge.

North Ridge Crib Goch

Stop at a point approximately 100m before, and 50m below, the base of the East Ridge (at the 700m contour line). From here, contour right, across rough ground, staying beneath the scree slopes of the Northeast Face. Initially, stay above a line of small broken crags. You are aiming for a flat-topped, grassy promontory (629 555), 250m north of the path and clearly visible on the other side of a vague hanging valley or bowl.

The promontory marks the start of the Fox's Path (page 186). Leave the promontory and head northwest, following a narrow path obliquely across the hillside. The path takes a gently rising line across the northeast face of Crib Goch, weaving in and out of the steep grassy runnels, to emerge on a small, grassy ledge, on the broad base of the North Ridge.

Description From Cwm Uchaf, ascend a short scree slope on the flank of the ridge to reach its slender crest. Or from the grassy ledge on the Fox's Path, head directly up steep grass, then scree, to reach the same point.

Walk easily up the crest of the ridge, which is wonderfully airy and a perfect, natural line. After 150m the crest becomes more pronounced and the drop to the left (east) becomes considerable. At this point, optional narrow paths appear just below the crest on the right (west). These are loose but okay.

A small rise on the crest of the ridge leads to a niche, from here on it's advisable to stick to the crest. Scramble directly out of the niche and continue along the now knife-edged ridge. Quartz blocks signal the end of the exposure and beyond which easy scrambling leads to the East Summit.

Descent or where next The most popular continuation is likely to be a traverse of the Main Ridge of Crib Goch (42). After which, a return to Pen-y-pass is possible by dropping south (left) from Bwlch Goch, the long grassy saddle between Crig Goch and Crib y Ddysgl, to reach the Pyg Track. The descent south from the bwlch is described on page 186.

Bwlch Goch can also be descended on its north side, allowing a traverse of the mountain that starts and finishes in the Llanberis Pass. Leave the grassy saddle at its lowest point, which is conspicuously eroded. An uncomplicated but scrappy scree slope leads back into Cwm Uchaf. The onward path into Cwm Glas Mawr follows a line that stays approximately 30m from the true right of the stream coming from Llyn Bach.

Robin Thomas crossing **Crib Goch's North Ridge** on a bitterly cold December day

A longer extension, creating an outing of over 2km of ridge walking and scrambling, is to traverse the Main Ridge, then continue along Crib y Ddysgl (43). Returning to Pen-y-pass via the Pyg Track or returning to the Llanberis Pass by descending the Cwm Glas Spur (45), which is described in the final two paragraphs on page 189.

A descent of the East Ridge (40) makes an excellent, shorter, and what could be considered 'alternative', traverse of the mountain. From the East Summit, walk east along the narrow crest of the ridge. Where it drops abruptly, veer to the true left, down shattered rock steps. At the end of the shattered red rock is a steeper band of rock. A wide depression provides the easiest passage through the band. Scramble down the depression, for approximately 60m, to reach a scruffy terrace.

The final rock steps can be descended at a number of possible places. Stay close to the blunt nose of the ridge to avoid loose ground. A well-used path then leads to Bwlch y Moch and the Pyg Track.

Tania Scotland on an evening's stroll, in early April, across **Crib Goch's Main Ridge**

Main Ridge Traverse

Crib Goch

42

Grade	1
Area	Snowdon Group
Aspect	East - West (910m)
Approach	85 mins (626 553)

One of the best ridge scrambles in Britain and synonymous with Welsh scrambling. Crossing this ridge has a magical quality, enhanced by the almost fantasy landscape within which it is set. It is an extraordinary place to be in the magic hours that bookend each day. The ridge is continuously narrow and extremely exposed. The northern flank has a near-vertical drop along its entire length, whilst the southern side is an unbroken sweep of steeply-angled terraces and cliffs. The scrambling is easy and is more of a head-thing than any physical challenge. The level of exposure shouldn't be underestimated.

Approach A conventional east to west crossing starts from the mountain's prominent East Summit. Both the East Ridge (40) and the North Ridge (41) lead directly to this summit. The East Ridge is generally considered the 'normal way' and is the quicker of the two routes.

Description From the East Summit, scoot west along the knife-edged arête. The rock along the very crest of the arête is solid and reliable. The vague paths that criss-cross lower down on the left (south) flank are tempting but rubbish. Stay off them.

After approximately 250m of airy scrambling, a gentle rise leads to a tiny cairn on the true summit. The cairn is so small that it is easily missed. A slight descent then leads to the three large pinnacles that guard the western end of the ridge.

Bypass the first two pinnacles on the left (south), curving back right, over scree-littered rocky terraces, into a wide gap on the ridge. Or, scramble directly over the pinnacles, at a slightly harder grade and with a tricky descent into the gap.

Math Roberts' evening run during a prolonged July heatwave

Dave Noddings crossing Crib Goch's Main Ridge on a brisk November day

Game over for conventional scrambling as Ali Thomas crosses Crib Goch after a heavy December snowfall

Main Ridge Traverse Crib Goch

Cross the short gap and ascend the third pinnacle by a slanting weakness on its right (north). Go over the pinnacle and scramble down on its left (south), via the most attractive looking line. Now veer back to a westerly direction and continue descending, over well-worn ground, to reach Bwlch Goch, the long grassy saddle before Crib y Ddysgl.

Descents or where next If continuing along Crib y Ddysgl (43), head west along a heavily eroded path. The path runs along the left (south) side of the broad grassy ridge and is the beginnings of the route.

The quickest way to return to Pen-y-pass is to head straight down the grassy slopes on the south side of the bwlch. These are steep at first but the gradient soon eases. The most comfortable line of descent is on the edge of a deep scree-filled rut. From the bottom of the rut, veer to the true right, down easy scree. A vague path then breaks off in the direction of the disused buildings on the shore of Glaslyn. Continue in this direction, down easy grass slopes, to meet with the Pyg Track.

To descend to the Llanberis Pass, drop down the north side of the bwlch, leaving the grassy saddle at its lowest point, which is conspicuously eroded. An uncomplicated but scrappy scree slope leads into Cwm Uchaf. Head northwest across the floor of the cwm to reach the descent path to Cwm Glas Mawr, which follows a line that stays approximately 30m on the true right of the stream coming from Llyn Bach. Once in Cwm Glas Mawr, a good path on the true left bank of the stream leads down to the Pass.

The Fox's Path is a devious path. It is a useful connection between the east side of Grib Goch and the north side of the mountain. The path starts on a flat-topped, grassy promontory (629 555), beneath the northeast face. From the promontory, it heads northwest, obliquely across the hillside. It then continues on a gently rising line across the northeast face, weaving in and out of the steep runnels, to emerge on a small, grassy ledge, on the broad base of the North Ridge. From the ledge, it contours around into Cwm Uchaf. In the reverse direction, its starting point in Cwm Uchaf (624 556) is difficult to locate.

The path is very narrow and at times, very exposed. Being on grass and dirt, it can be slippery when wet and there is nothing to hold on to. It is not a 'family path' or a route for the inexperienced.

Crib y Ddysgl

Garnedd Ugain / Crib y Ddysgl

43

Grade	1
Area	Snowdon Group
Aspect	East - West (905m)
Approach	110 mins (621 551)

A lofty mix of scrambling and walking across a long, well-defined ridge. This is the natural continuation of a traverse of Crib Goch and the second stage on the classic round of the Snowdon Horseshoe. As a consequence of its long-standing popularity, the crest of the ridge is eroded and shattered, with numerous scrappy paths along its flanks doing their best to avoid any exposure. Somehow, none of this detracts from the enjoyment of crossing such a cool, high-level ridge.

Approach Crib y Ddysgl is nearly always gained by first ascending either the East Ridge (40) or North Ridge (41) of Crib Goch, followed by a traverse of the mountain's Main Ridge (42). The route is then started from Bwlch Goch, the long grassy saddle between Crib Goch and Crib y Ddysgl.

There is no reason why Crib y Ddysgl can't be ascended on its own, without the necessity of first crossing Crib Goch. The approach for this option involves a fair amount of steep walking, with the final push up to Bwlch Goch being particularly hard-going. But this is more than compensated by the unique scenery and seclusion found in Cwm Glas and Cwm Uchaf, the two high mountain cwms through which this approach route weaves.

Park at one of the large lay-bys (621 571), situated on both sides of the road, below Clogwyn y Grochan, in the Lanberis Pass. Cross the river using the nearby small vehicular bridge at Blaen-y-nant (623 570) and continue straight ahead. After 50m, turn right over a second bridge and head up a good path on the right (west) side of the stream.

Paul James crossing a deserted **Crib y Ddysgyl** on a windy late December day

Follow the right (west) bank of the river across Cwm Glas Mawr towards the impressive crags beneath Cyrn Las. A steep stony path picks a way up the hillside to the left of crags. Head up the path and, at the top of the rise, veer left towards Llyn Glas, a small lake with an island, nestled in the entrance to Cwm Uchaf.

At the lake, head southeast into the catchment of Cwm Uchaf. From the highest and most southerly point on the cwm floor, follow a rough zig-zag path that climbs steeply up towards Bwlch Goch.

Description From Bwlch Goch, head west along a heavily eroded path, which runs along the left (south) side of the initial section of grassy ridge. Where the ridge rears up, tackle it direct, avoiding the path on the left.

A second, more impressive rise, this time rocky, is also taken direct. Or, skirt to the left and scramble into a large bay of jumbled blocks and corners, then gain the crest by the most enticing line. Continue along the now gently-angled ridge to the summit trig point. The most rewarding line is along the shattered crest, avoiding the scrappy paths that litter the ridge's right flank.

Garnedd Ugain / Crib y Ddysgl **Crib y Ddysgl**

Descents or where next The most likely descent routes, if returning to Pen-y-pass, would be either the Pyg Track or Miners Track. Both these tracks start at the finger stone at Bwlch Glas, the lowest point between Crib Y Ddysgl and Snowdon.

If continuing on the classic circuit of the Snowdon Horseshoe, head southwest to join the unmistakably wide Llanberis Path, which runs adjacent to the mountain railway and leads directly to Snowdon's summit.

From the summit buildings, descend southwest for a distance of 150m, until the finger stone marking the top of the Watkin Path. From the finger stone, bail southeast down the zig-zags and follow the path to Bwlch y Saethau, a grassy flattening beneath Snowdon's East Ridge. A direct descent of the East Ridge isn't recommended, as too much erosion and loose scree makes it, let's say, disagreeable.

Continue southeast on a good path, or better still, scramble along the undulating ridge on your left, to reach Bwlch Ciliau; the lowest point between Snowdon and Lliwedd, and the junction where the Watkin Path drops right (southwest), into Cwm Llan. From the Bwlch, follow the Traverse of Lliwedd (48) and that route's descent, north into Cwm Dyli, to meet with the Miners Track.

If returning to the Llanberis Pass, a descent of the Cwm Glas Spur (45), the ridge between Cwm Glas Mawr and Cwm Glas Bach, is a direct, scenic and uncomplicated route. From the summit trig point on Crib y Ddysgl, head north down easy grass slopes, skirting the edge of Cwm Glas, to reach the promontory (612 559) above the upper cliffs of Cyrn Las.

From the grassy promontory, follow a faint but discernible path northeast as it heads down the crest of the spur. At the top of a steepening, scramble down an eroded recess on the true left, then down scree. A short stretch of path then traverses to the true right, across the hillside, back to the crest of the spur. A second steepening is also avoided by a recess on the true left. A short zig-zag path then leads back to the now broader crest of the spur. Continue easily down the grassy spur and at the most attractive opportunity, break right into Cwm Glas Mawr.

The long crest of the **Clogwyn y Person Arête** and the cliffs of Clogwyn y Ddysgl

Sarah Ridgway at the end of the difficulties on a fast evening ascent of the **Clogwyn y Person Arête**

Clogwyn y Person Arête

Crib y Ddysgl

44

Grade	3
Area	Snowdon Group
Aspect	Northeast (730m)
Approach	70 mins (616 555)

A compelling scramble that ascends one of the strongest natural lines in all the Welsh mountains. The arête shoots straight down from the ridge of Crib y Ddysgl, creating a striking feature as it splits the mountain's northern cwms. Like many great mountaineering objectives, it is a difficult route to escape from; huge cliffs form its right flank and dangerously chossy ground falls steeply to its left. The rock quality along the crest of the arête is generally sound; the situations throughout are magnificent and considering this is a ridge line, the scrambling is surprisingly varied.

Approach The most direct and by far the most scenic approach starts in the Llanberis Pass. Park at one of the large lay-bys (621 571) situated on both sides of the road, below Clogwyn y Grochan. Cross the river using the nearby small road bridge at Blaen-y-nant (623 570) and continue straight ahead. After 50m, turn right over a second bridge and head up a grassy path on the right (west) side of the stream.

Follow the right (west) bank of the river across Cwm Glas Mawr towards the impressive crags beneath Cyrn Las. A steep stony path picks a way up the hillside to the left of crags. Head up the path and, at the top of the rise, continue over a few smaller rises into the catchment of Cwm Glas.

The Clogwyn y Person arête stands dominant on the left. The huge cliffs of Clogwyn y Ddysgl fall down from its crest and create a definitive left boundary of the cwm. Aim for the toe of the arête; a slabby snout of rock known as the Parson's Nose.

The arête can also be approached via the Fox's Path (page 186). From where the path enters Cwm Uchaf (624 556), curve clock-wise around the undulating floor of the cwm to reach the Parson's Nose (can be tricky in poor visibility).

Clogwyn y Person Arête   Crib y Ddysgl

Description The slabby buttress of the Parson's Nose is separated from the main bulk of the arête by a gully, Western Gully, which leads up to a niche. Scramble into the rocky confines of the gully and after 25 metres or so, head diagonally up and right, following a series of ledges and short, steep walls. This leads to a scruffy terrace, roughly level with the top of the nose.

From the terrace upwards, if the crest of the arête is tackled directly, with all walls and obstacles taken more or less front on, this will be a stiff and challenging grade 3 scramble. There wouldn't be much dissimilarity with what you'd expect to encounter on an AD alpine ridge.

Weaving around the blunt arête, seeking out the way of least resistance, is just as much fun. With a keen sense of route finding the scramble can be reduced to grade 2, but still with a fair degree of excitement.

Eventually the angle of the arête eases and the terrain becomes more broken. The scrambling interest slowly peters out but the situation always remains impressive. The route finishes along a scree-covered spur, which merges into the summit slopes of Crib y Ddysgl.

Descents or where next The summit of Crib y Ddysgl would be the obvious and fine culmination to the scramble. A descent of the Cwm Glas Spur (45), the ridge between Cwm Glas Mawr and Cwm Glas Bach, would then lead directly back to the Llanberis Pass. From the flattening at the top of the arête, head west, up the final section of Crib y Ddysgl (43), to reach the summit trig point. From the summit, head north down easy grass slopes, skirting the edge of Cwm Glas, to reach the promontory (612 559) above the upper cliffs of Cyrn Las.

From the grassy promontory, follow a faint but discernible path northeast as it heads down the crest of the spur. At the top of a steepening, scramble down an eroded recess on the true left, then down scree. A short stretch of path then traverses to the true right, across the hillside, back to the crest of the spur. A second steepening is also avoided by a recess on the true left. A short zig-zag path then leads back to the now broader crest of the spur. Continue easily down the grassy spur and at the most attractive opportunity, break right into Cwm Glas Mawr.

Libby Peter sussing a way around the lower section of the **Clogwyn y Person Arête**

One of the best scrambling enchainments in North Wales is to continue with a circuit of Cwm Uchaf; descending Crib y Ddysgl (43), crossing the Main Ridge of Crib Goch (42), then heading down the mountain's North Ridge (41). A spectacular excursion. From the flattening at the top of the Clogwyn y Person Arête, head east, down Crib Y Ddysgl. This is straightforward except for one steep step, 200m before Bwlch Goch, which is easiest on the true right. The west to east crossing of Crib Goch's Main Ridge is also straightforward. The initial pinnacle is surmounted on its right and descended on it's true left, into a wide gap. The remaining pinnacles are turned on the right; a well-worn route is very easy to follow and rejoins the crest immediately after the pinnacles.

From Crib Goch's East Summit, head north, sticking to the crest of the knife-edged ridge. The knife-edge is short lived. However, there is a short, exposed down-climb into a niche before the broader, easier section of the ridge can be reached. Walk down the shattered crest of the ridge, stopping approximately 50m before its natural end. From here, a well-used scree path on the true left flank drops into Cwm Uchaf. Head west across the floor of the cwm to reach the initial approach path coming from Cwm Glas Mawr, which follows a line that stays approximately 30m from the true right of the stream coming from Llyn Bach.

Libby Peter and Paul James taking a straight line up the **Clogwyn y Person Arête**

Cwm Glas Spur

Crib y Ddysgl / Llanberis Pass

45

Grade	1-
Area	Llanberis Pass
Aspect	Northeast (510m)
Approach	30 mins (616 566)

A sheep in wolf's clothing. The Cwm Glas Spur is the long ridge separating Cwm Glas Mawr and Cwm Glas Bach. A prominent pyramidal buttress, Cyrn Las, forms its upper section. It is a far easier proposition than its imposing appearance from the valley would suggest. In fact, it is little more than a scrambly path. The spur is secluded and feels un-trodden. It is a beautiful and quiet route to the summits of Crib y Ddysgl and Snowdon, which can be busy mountains if ascended by any of the conventional walking paths. The spur also provides a scenic and uncomplicated descent.

Approach The broad toe of the spur can be accessed directly from the road in the Llanberis Pass. However, a slight detour into Cwm Glas Mawr makes a more interesting journey. Park at one of the large lay-bys (621 571) situated on both sides of the road, below Clogwyn y Grochan. Cross the river using the nearby small road bridge at Blaen-y-nant (623 570) and continue straight ahead. After 50m, turn right over a second bridge and head up a grassy path on the right (west) side of the stream (map on page 168).

As the path levels out onto the floor of Cwm Glas Mawr, it passes between two van-sized boulders, the right one of which is split. Continue for a further 200m, to a large, solitary quartz-faced boulder. It's worth giving a few minutes here, to soak up the atmosphere of this impressive cwm. From the boulder, head northwest and strike up grassy slopes to gain the skyline.

Description Walk up the grassy ridge to a level area. Above, the ridge rises up as a steep nose of broken rock. Bypass the nose by going around to the right (west) and following a zig-zag path into and up a natural recess. Alternatively, the nose can be ascended directly, but care is needed with loose and dirty rock.

Calum Muskett on a muggy evening's run up the grassy paths of the **Cwm Glas Spur**

The scenic approach route to the **Cwm Glas Spur**

Cyrn Las

45

Cwm Glas Mawr

Crib y Ddysgl / Llanberis Pass — Cwm Glas Spur

Continue up the ridge to a second, steeper nose of broken rock. From its base, take a gently rising, rightward traverse across the hillside, along a lovely stretch of path. At the end of the short traverse cut back up and left, following a scrambly path, initially over scree, then up an eroded recess, to eventually regain the crest of the ridge. The crest leads to a grassy promontory at the top of the spur.

Descents or where next For the summit of Crib y Ddysgl, head south, up easy grass slopes, skirting the cliffs above Cwm Glas. To then continue to Snowdon, head southwest to join the unmistakably wide Llanberis Path, which runs adjacent to the mountain railway and leads directly to the summit.

The best descent options, particularly if you'd like to maintain the very easy grade of the day, are via either the Pyg Track or Miners Track. Both these tracks start at the finger stone at Bwlch Glas, the lowest point between Crib y Ddysgl and Snowdon, and both lead to Pen-y-pass at the head of the Llanberis Pass. The Pyg Track is the higher and more direct route. The Miners Track is slightly easier going, has some quite special lakeside sections and only takes an additional half-hour or so to complete.

For an excellent long mountain excursion, in keeping with the overall easy scrambling grade of the day, continue over Snowdon and then press on with a traverse of Lliwedd (48). This would essentially create a technically easier alternative to the established circuit of the Snowdon Horseshoe. It would still have all the Horseshoe atmosphere but avoids the exposure on the ridges of Crib Goch and Crib y Ddysgl. Plus the added benefit of having visited the wilder, less-frequented northern cwms of Crib y Ddysgl.

From Snowdon's summit buildings, descend southwest for a distance of 150m, until the finger stone marking the top of the Watkin Path. From the finger stone, bail southeast down the zig-zags and follow the path to Bwlch y Saethau; a grassy flattening beneath Snowdon's East Ridge. A direct descent of the East Ridge isn't recommended, as too much erosion and loose scree makes it, let's say, disagreeable.

Continue southeast on a good path, or better still, scramble along the undulating ridge on your left, to reach Bwlch Ciliau; the lowest point between Snowdon and Lliwedd, and the junction where the Watkin Path drops right, into Cwm Llan. From the Bwlch, follow the Traverse of Lliwedd (48) and that route's descent, north into Cwm Dyli, to meet with the Miners Track.

Toby Keep nipping up warm rock on **Llechog Buttress**

Llechog Buttress

Crib y Ddysgl / Llanberis Pass

46

Grade	2
Area	Llanberis Pass
Aspect	Northeast (545m)
Approach	35 mins (608 569)

Good for blowing away the cobwebs This prominent buttress sits at the top of the west bounding rib of Cwm Glas Bach, an unfrequented but easily accessed cwm in the northeast corner of the Snowdon range. The crest of the buttress looks extremely promising from the valley floor but proves to be quite short and discontinuous. However, the brevity of scrambling is more than compensated for by the commanding views of the Llanberis Pass and the quirkiness of the Snowdon locomotives criss-crossing the skyline of the cwm.

Approach Park at Nant Peris and walk southeast for 1km, along the A4086, through Gwastadnant. For part of this distance there is a footpath and boardwalk construction on the south side of the road. Alternatively, park in the Llanberis Pass, at the large lay-by (621 571) directly below Clogwyn y Grochan. From here, walk northwest for 900m towards Gwastadnant (map on page 168).

Cross the bridge over the river (614 576) and follow a vehicular track past a dwelling (be considerate concerning noise). At the end of the track, head straight up the hillside, aiming for a low-profile rocky spur. This easy-angled spur leads directly to a perched block at the base of Llechog Buttress.

Description Behind the perched block is a steep 10m barrier with a leftward leaning groove at its centre. The groove is enticing but turns out to be too difficult (and awkward to down climb if you've been inquisitive). Instead, scramble up a grassy runnel on the left, containing a flat-topped chockstone. Step right from the top of the chockstone and continue upwards, arbitrarily linking as many ribs and rock steps as possible, to eventually arrive at a grassy platform.

Llechog Buttress from the approach along the Llanberis Pass

Toby Keep with a huge slice of his favourite cheese

Crib y Ddysgl / Llanberis Pass — Llechog Buttress

Above the grassy platform is a melange of large blocks, above which the buttress rears up steeply. Climb a tricky leftward leaning groove at the rear the platform. From the top of the groove, head up a grassy break, or scramble up the clean rib on its left, until confronted by a wedged rectangular block. Heave over the stuck block. Then trend up and right over larger blocks to a boulder-strewn platform below a 15m vertical wall.

To the right of the wall is an obvious recess, which culminates in a v-shaped groove. Scramble up the right-bounding rib of the recess. Then trend right, into a much more friendly looking groove. Ascend this easier-angled groove for a few metres, then cut back left along an exposed stepped ramp, to regain the crest of the buttress. All route finding difficulties are now over. Easy, enjoyable scrambling leads to a good viewpoint at the top of the buttress.

Descents or where next From the top of the buttress the quickest descent is to head right (northwest), along the cliff top, to a small promontory (marked as a 610m spot-height). This promontory is the top of a spur forming the right-hand boundary of Cwm Beudy Mawr; the cwm directly above Gwastadnant. Cross a small stile and head northeast, down a faint grassy path. The path soon cuts back right, before zig-zagging steeply down into the cwm.

As the path enters the lower part of the cwm, it begins to lose identity and is difficult to follow. Either head across open, rough ground, back towards the toe of the low-profile spur used on the approach. Or, continue downhill, veering to the true left, to reach a path, which runs alongside the main riverbank. Head northeast along the riverside to a footbridge (608 579), which gives access back to the A4086.

A more rewarding descent is to skirt around the top of Cwm Glas Bach and drop down the Cwm Glas Spur (45). From the top of Llechog buttress, walk left (southeast), along the cliff tops, to reach the grassy promontory (612 559) above the cliffs of Cyrn Las. Follow a faint but discernible path northeast as it heads down the crest of the spur. At the top of a steepening, scramble down an eroded recess on the true left, then down scree. A short stretch of path then traverses to the true right, across the hillside, back to the crest of the spur. A second steepening is also avoided by a recess on the true left. A short zig-zag path then leads back to the now broader crest of the spur. Continue easily down the grassy spur and at the most attractive opportunity, break right into Cwm Glas Mawr.

The magnificent setting of Y Gribin, curving up beneath Snowdon's Trinity Face

Y Gribin

Snowdon / Lliwedd

47

Grade	1
Area	Snowdon Group
Aspect	Northeast (620m)
Approach	65 mins (619 545)

A lovely little scramble in a magical setting, nestled in the centre of a landscape of copper-green lakes and towering peaks… trippy but true. The route ascends the short but pronounced ridge separating Glaslyn and Llyn Llydaw. The quality of the rock is okay but has a tendency to be greasy after long periods of rain. It is better in dry conditions but not impossible in the wet. With a significant proportion of the approach and descent being on constructed paths, it is also an easy scramble to run.

Approach Park at Pen-y-pass (car park usually full by 8am at weekends) or in the free lay-bys (665 559) on the A4086, east of the Pen-y-Gwryd Hotel, just over the Conwy County border. There is also a park-and-ride scheme operating from Nant Peris but the timetable is very limited outside peak holiday periods.

For a shortened high-level approach, head west from Pen-y-pass along the Pyg Track, to the prominent col of Bwlch y Moch. The bwlch is where the path to Crib Goch splits off. It is also the first viewpoint for Snowdon, Lliwedd and Llyn Llydaw. Continue along the Pyg Track, which is the lower, left-hand path that contours around the hillside.

After 1.5 kilometres, the path arrives at two large cairns and takes a sharp right turn to the northwest. From this point continue southwest, down an easy grass slope on a vague path, towards Glaslyn. On reaching the Miners Track, turn left and walk the short distance to the outflow of Glaslyn.

A slightly longer approach, but with a lake-side flavour and more easy-going if running, is to follow the Miners Track from Pen-y-pass. Cross the causeway and continue around the northern edge of the Llyn Llydaw. The track then climbs slowly up to the outflow of Glaslyn.

Sarah Ridgway, Libby Peter, Fly and Bella make their way up **Y Gribin** en route to Lliwedd

Chris Wright looking out across Llyn Llydaw from the quartz-topped pinnacle on Lliwedd's West Buttress

Snowdon / Lliwedd Y Gribin

Cross the outflow stream to the remnants of an old dam. A faint path then gently rises diagonally up the hillside on the left. After passing beneath a large rectangular boulder, the path cuts uphill to reach a col on the skyline. Head southwest, up to a flattening below the steep part of the ridge.

Description Ascend slabs slightly to the right of the crest. Once back on the crest, and faced with a steep drop on the left (east), scramble rightwards up a series of worn grooves and steps.

Continue up the ridge, over similar terrain, interspersed by sections of rough scree-covered path. The best line never detours too far from the crest. A small cairn on a grassy promontory marks an abrupt end to the ridge.

Descents or where next The natural continuation, and probably the quickest way back to Pen-y-pass, is to cross over Lliwedd. From the top of Y Gribin, walk south to meet the Watkin Path. Head southeast along the path, or better still, scramble along the undulating ridge on your left to reach Bwlch Ciliau; the lowest point between Snowdon and Lliwedd, and the junction where the Watkin Path drops right, into Cwm Llan. From the Bwlch, follow the Traverse of Lliwedd (48) and that route's descent, north into Cwm Dyli, to meet with the Miners Track.

To take in Snowdon's summit, head southwest from the top of Y Gribin then, at a small pool, veer right to Bwlch y Saethau; the flattening beneath Snowdon's east ridge. Despite being hideously eroded, it's still just about possible to ascend the East Ridge, but only if there are no other parties above you. Far safer is to head west, up the zig-zags on the Watkin Path, to the finger stone at the intersection with the South Ridge. From there, it's a short walk to the summit buildings.

To return to Pen-y-pass from Snowdon's summit, reverse your ascent of the Watkin Path, then continue over Lliwedd (48), as previously described. Alternatively, walk northwest on the Llanberis Path to the finger stone at Bwlch Glas, the lowest point between Snowdon and Crib Y Ddysgl. From there the Pyg Track and Miners Track start their descent.

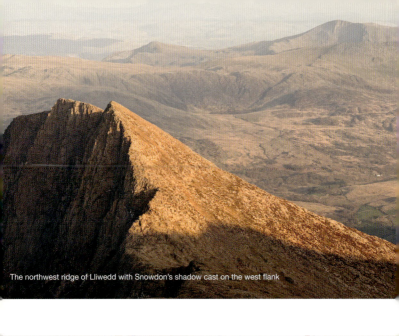
The northwest ridge of Lliwedd with Snowdon's shadow cast on the west flank

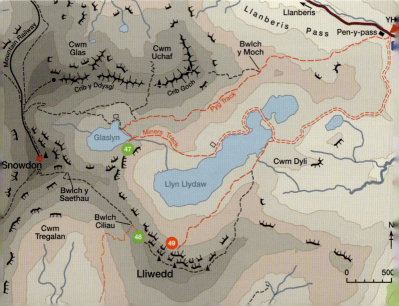

Lliwedd Traverse

Lliwedd

48

Grade	1-
Area	Snowdon Group
Aspect	Northwest - Northeast (744m)
Approach	100 mins (619 537)

An easy and dramatic scramble, which skirts along the top of the biggest cliffs in Wales. The frequent glimpses and close proximity of the mountain's huge northeast cliffs create a real sense of mountaineering adventure but with no exposure and no necessity to go near any big drops. The traverse of Lliwedd (893m) is most often undertaken as the final section in the circuit of the Snowdon Horseshoe. It is definitely worth doing in its own right and should never be considered as just the last leg of anything. The route also makes a good high-level run.

Approach There are a number of possible approaches to this scramble. The most dramatic and logical is to first ascend Y Gribin (47) and is described on page 203. This entails a walk along the north shore of Llyn Llydaw, from where you'll see Lliwedd on its best side and get a full appreciation of the scale of the mountain's northeast cliffs.

In keeping with the very easy grade of this scramble, a long but incredibly scenic approach starts with an ascent of the Cwm Glas Spur (45), then continues over Snowdon. This approach begins in the Llanberis Pass and is described on page 195.

If you are traversing Lliwedd as part of the circuit of the Snowdon Horseshoe, the preceding scramble on this classic outing is Crib y Ddysgl (43) and is described on page 187.

It is also possible to approach Lliwedd from the south, using the Watkin Path. Take the A498 Capel Curig to Beddgelert road and park at either of the parking areas in Nant Gwynant (628 507), 1.5km after passing Llyn Gwynant. Start at the stone steps located 60m southwest from where the A498 crosses the Afon Glaslyn river.

Winter conditions can even linger into late April as Anne Robertson heads for the northwest ridge of Lliwedd

Lliwedd **Lliwedd Traverse**

Climb the stone steps and head north along a woodland footpath. After 450m the footpath emerges from the woods onto a wider cart/vehicular track. Follow the track as it curves sharply to the northwest to enter an open cwm. The track then curves in a clockwise direction around the cwm, before climbing up to the left (west) of the Afon Cwm Llan river above some attractive waterfalls (a good swimming spot on a hot day).

Continue up the track to the flat floor of Cwm Llan. The well-established track then crosses the river and skirts around the north side of the cwm to reach an area of old quarry workings. From here the Watkin Path heads north, rising obliquely beneath the west flank of Lliwedd, before turning sharply east and climbing up to Bwlch Ciliau.

Description Start at Bwlch Ciliau; the lowest point between Snowdon and Lliwedd. From the bwlch, ascend the northwest ridge of Lliwedd (head southeast!). The best scrambling, over short walls and steps, is on the left, overlooking Llyn Llydaw. An easy, almost walking path runs up to the right. Continue up the broad crest of the ridge, without any complication, to the lovely West Summit.

Stay on the broad rocky crest, over the East Summit, before swinging northeast over the minor summit of Lliwedd Bach. An eroded path then drops down the true right flank of the hill, to reach a sizeable grassy flattening.

Descent or where next To return to Pen-y-pass, drop north from a gap (631 535) at the northern end of the flattening. A steep, rough path veers to the true right, down the hillside. As the gradient eases, the quality of the path improves. Continue along the east shore of Llyn Llydaw, to the corrugated-iron valve house. From here, walk east along the Miners Track to Pen-y-pass.

The descent to Nant Gwynant is off-piste but is not difficult to navigate. From the flattening at the base of the ridge, head southeast, straight down the fall-line of Lliwedd's grassy slopes. After dropping approximately 150m, you'll arrive at an area of disused quarry workings (633 532). From the lowest quarry workings, a good path heads southwest, obliquely down the hillside. Follow the path, through a small area of woodland, into lower Cwm Llan. Cross the river at a bridge and head up the opposite bank to pick up the original approach track. Walk south down the track to Nant Gwynant.

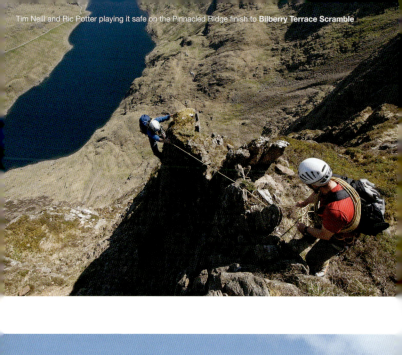

Tim Neill and Ric Potter playing it safe on the Pinnacled Ridge finish to **Bilberry Terrace Scramble**

Lliwedd's northeast cliffs

East Buttress

Central Gully

West Buttress

49

Bilberry Terrace Scramble

Lliwedd

49

Grade	3+
Area	Snowdon Group
Aspect	Northeast (650m)
Approach	60 mins (624 534)

A magnificent outing and by far the most committing undertaking described in this book. The route weaves an intricate line up Lliwedd's huge West Buttress, with situations and atmosphere akin to an alpine face. The rock is generally solid, except for a few shattered blocks within the final 100m. The entire scramble catches the early morning sun and is best attempted following a few days of dry weather (the difficult sections are likely to feel desperate if wet). This is a fantastic scramble… but one which could easily turn into an epic.

Approach Park at Pen-y-pass (car park usually full by 8am at weekends) or in the free lay-bys (665 559) on the A4086, east of the Pen-y-Gwryd Hotel, just over the Conwy County border. There is also a park-and-ride scheme operating from Nant Peris but the timetable is very limited outside peak holiday periods.

From Pen-y-pass follow the Miners Track to the corrugated-iron valve house on the edge of Llyn Llydaw. From here, turn left and follow the path hugging the shoreline to the bridge crossing the lake's outflow. Continue southeast along the now rising path for 200m (this is the main descent path from Lliwedd) until meeting a junction with a narrower path heading out right.

Head along the narrow path as it contours underneath the left-hand side of the cliffs and begins to pick its way up through small bluffs. The track soon loses a singular identity and breaks off into numerous vague tracks. Aim for the scree slope under Central Gully, the depression separating East and West Buttresses (the two largest buttresses).

Bilberry Terrace Scramble   Lliwedd

Description Head up the scree fan beneath Central Gully. From the top of the fan, veer up and right to a well-used ledge below a rock barrier, which guards the lower left end of Bilberry Terrace. For reference, 30m further down to the right, at the base of the rock barrier, is a distinctive quartz-topped block.

Scramble rightwards up a 20m high gangway. This consists of a series of rocky steps, the top one of which is a bit tricky. Gain the wide grassy terrace and follow it easily as it rises rightwards for 75m to the foot of a steep corner.

Ascend the 5m corner, which is surprisingly tricky, then continue up more easily for a further 6m, trending left, to a platform and a spike belay.

Cut back right, over an exposed slab to reach another platform. Ascend a short, wide crack, then continue traversing along the terrace. After a few metres veer left up a steep-ish groove, which rises rightwards underneath a smooth, copper coloured wall. From the top of this rocky groove, regain the terrace on the right.

Continue along the terrace, passing a gully with a wedged plinth at half height, to reach a notch formed by a pinnacle. This is Pinnacle Corner, where the terrace crosses the central ridge of the buttress and overlooks a wide arc of the cliff.

Continue rightwards for approximately 30m, crossing some spookily thin grassy ledges and passing a cannon stone, until a rib of rock signals the natural end of the terrace. Cut sharply back left and head up some well-worn steps for 25m, leading into a 15m wide depression.

Ascend the depression on its right, following some well-kicked steps in the vegetation. Trend left towards the top of the depression (passing a spike) and exit using a leftward sloping plinth. Continue traversing left to regain the central ridge of the buttress at a point approximately 30m above Pinnacle Corner.

Cross another wide depression by descending slightly and then scrambling diagonally up, aiming for a notch on the ridge to the left. Continue for a further 30m, on a rising leftwards traverse along a rocky ledge, to reach the crest of a yet another ridge (look for a quartz and moss topped pinnacle).

Cut back up and right, to reach the base of a rocky groove with a spike just to its left. Ascend the rocky groove that culminates in a steep chimney, to reach the foot of a 40m wide depression.

Tim Neill cutting across Lliwedd's West Buttress high up on **Bilberry Terrace Scramble**

Pick a way up the depression, veering left near its top, to emerge directly on the summit. Or better still, traverse horizontally left to gain the base of a pinnacled ridge that is 'crying out to be climbed'. Carefully ascend the shattered ridge. Both these finishes need care with suspect rock.

Descent or where next The quickest descent is to head southeast over the East Peak then swing northeast over the minor summit of Lliwedd Bach. Continue down an eroded path, on the true right flank of the hill, to a sizeable flattening. From a gap (631 535) at the northern end of the flattening, drop north down a steep, rough path. The path veers to the true right and meets up with the original approach route, a short distance above Llyn Llydaw.

An easy descent of Lliwedd's northwest ridge, followed by a scrambly descent of Y Gribin (47), rounds off a day nicely. From the northern shore of Llyn Llydaw you'll get a clear view of the entire line of the Bilberry Terrace scramble. The top of Y Gribin is located 125m northeast of the small pool at Bwlch y Saethau; the large flat area beneath Snowdon's east ridge. The descent is generally easier and safer by sticking to the true left flank of the ridge. Continue along the Miners Track back to Pen-y-pass.

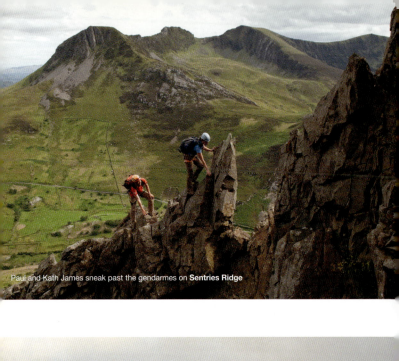
Paul and Kath James sneak past the gendarmes on **Sentries Ridge**

The cliffs of Craig y Bera on the south flank of Mynydd Mawr

Sentries Ridge

Mynydd Mawr

50

Grade	2+
Area	Nantlle
Aspect	South (420m)
Approach	45 mins (546 540)

A scramble that oozes atmosphere. It ascends one of the long shattered ridges that sweep down the southern flank of Mynydd Mawr; a small but attractive mountain that sits on its own, to the west of the main ranges. The ridge is narrow and exposed in places with a distinct air of seriousness, heightened by the loose and often tottering nature of its rock. The scrambling is not particularly difficult but does require a 'switched on' approach at all times. There is a certain charm to this scramble, which also applies to the lonely summit of Mynydd Mawr.

Approach Sentries Ridge lies within Craig y Bera; the maze of ridges and shattered buttresses that cap the south flank of Mynydd Mawr. The crag is clearly visible from the stretch of B4418 road that runs between Rhyd-Ddu and Nantle.

Take the A4085, Caernarfon to Beddgelert road, and park at the Snowdon Ranger Youth Hostel (565 551). From the hostel, walk south along the road for 1km, to the Planwydd campsite and farm (568 539). From the campsite gate, walk past the buildings then follow a footpath across the field on the left. Continue in the same direction through the woods until the edge of the plantation is reached.

Alternatively, park at Rhyd Ddu. From just north of the Cwellyn Arms pub, walk up the B4418 road, signposted for Nantlle. After 100m, at the end of the houses, turn right onto a forestry track. Continue along the forestry track for 1km until an intersection with a waymarked footpath; the footpath that starts at the Planwydd Campsite. Then turn left and, as above, follow the footpath up to the edge of the plantation.

Kath James sniffs out the best route on the steep upper ribs of **Sentries Ridge**

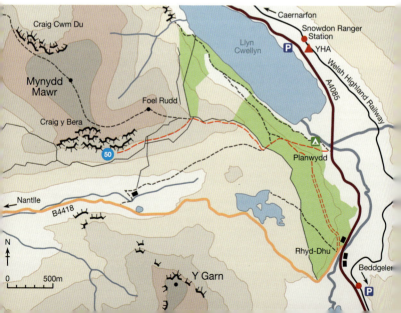

Mynydd Mawr **Sentries Ridge**

At the edge of the plantation, turn right and follow the grassy path uphill, tracing the tree line (some recent felling at the time of writing this guide), until the highest group of trees on the hillside.

Cross the stile over the fence that comes in from the left. From just beyond the stile, at the corner of the plantation, follow a faint path that heads left (southwest) and contours around the south side of the mountain. The path initially crosses steep grassy slopes before reaching two adjacent stiles, crossing over a fence and then a dilapidated wall. The path then continues across scree, passing beneath the cliffs of Craig y Bera.

Description Start in the large recess situated to the right of the lowest buttress of Craig y Bera. The truncated foot of Sentries Ridge is situated in the centre of this recess and is flanked on either side by a wide scree-filled gully.

The foot of the ridge consists of a vertical 5m high rock wall. Bypass this wall using the gully on either the left or right, then at the first opportunity scramble up to reach the heather-covered crest of the ridge.

Pick your way up a scrappy slab to reach a ledge below the first significant steepening. Turn the steepening on the left and scramble up broken rocks to regain the crest. This is where the true character of the route reveals itself.

Walk (or shuffle) along the now extremely narrow ridge to reach a gendarme. This is turned on the right, with an up close and intimate manoeuvre, to reach the sanctuary of a small notch.

Rising up behind the notch is a large tower. Either swing around the tower on the right or bypass it more easily on the left. A short way beyond the tower is a spacious and comfortable bilberry-covered col.

The way ahead involves a sequence of interlinking ribs and it is very much a 'follow your nose' affair. Rising up from the bilberry-covered col is a well-defined rocky rib. Scramble up the rib to reach a second col. Another, shorter rib then leads up to a rocky notch with an unusual tunnel. Behind the notch is an even steeper rib. Head directly up this to a further col. Continue up the remainder of the ridge, over rocky pinnacles, to reach the top of the crag.

Sentries Ridge   Mynnyd Mawr

Descents or where next It would be a crime not to visit the lovely summit of this isolated mountain. Head northwest, up a broad grassy spur, to arrive at the summit cairn in less than 10 minutes. The reward is a superb 360 degree panorama; with views to all the main ranges, both the north and west coasts, and on a clear day, even as far as the Cumbrian Fells and across the Irish Sea to the Wicklow Mountains.

To descend from the summit, head southeast, down the broad grassy spur. Above Craig y Bera, swing northeast and walk down the path to the small cairn at Foel Rudd. From the cairn, the path descends east, back to the highest point of the plantation, from where you can re-trace your approach, back down to the valley.

Classic Link-ups

The classic link-ups One of the great things about scrambling in North Wales is the ease with which routes can be linked together to create a longer outing. Moving from one scramble to the next is arguably the most satisfying and natural way to travel in these mountains.

The following link-ups are widely accepted as the best in Snowdonia and are up there among the most prized scrambling journeys in Britain. Each of their constituent scrambles has already been described separately. Within those descriptions, specifically in the paragraphs outlining the descent options, you'll find all the information needed for navigating around these classic traverses.

The Snowdon Horseshoe	40 East Ridge of Crib Goch
	42 Main Ridge of Crib Goch
	43 Crib y Ddysgl
	- a traverse of Snowdon
	48 Lliwedd Traverse
The Cwm Bochlwyd Horseshoe	12 North Ridge of Tryfan
	17 South Ridge of Tryfan *descent*
	18 Bristly Ridge
	24 Y Gribin *descent*
The Cwm Uchaf Circuit	44 Clogwyn y Person Arête
	43 Crib y Ddysgl *descent*
	42 Main Ridge of Crib Goch
	41 North Ridge of Crib Goch *descent*

Streaky Desroy cruising along the upper section of the **Dolmen Ridge**

Calling the following link-up a classic would be stretching it a bit. But it does excel in both quality and quantity of scrambling, and in the sheer variety of situations it throws up. It is a trip around the northern cwms of the Glyders taking in some of the strongest and most interesting lines in the Ogwen Valley. Although it appears to meander around, it is a surprisingly logical journey that always seems to flow. It is simply a superb day out.

The Northern Cwms of the Glyders

- **31** Idwal Buttress and Continuation
- **26** Cneifion Arête
- **25** Y Gribin True Start *part descent*
- **23** Dolmen Ridge
- **18** Bristly Ridge *descent*
- **06** Pinnacle Scramble

Notes

Notes

Notes